the
audio-
visual
man

THE AUDIO- VISUAL MAN

**edited by
Pierre Babin**

translated by

C. Belisle
C. Dozois
U. Duchesneau
J. Green
S. MacDonald
F. McMahon

PFLAUM   DAYTON, OHIO   1970

Photo Credits:
National Film Board of Canada: pp.
44, 72, 84, 112, 122, 138, 146-147, 148,
185, 198
United States Information Service
(USIS): pp. 2, 6, 30, 38, 93
UNESCO: pp. vi, 10, 54, 210
Thompson-CSF: pp. 12, 28, 36-37
UPI Photo: pp. 14, 79, 183
Rene Bouillot: pp. 21, 68-69, 196
Palnic-Gunter R. Reitz: pp. 102, 116
Ville de Montreal: pp. 108, 150
Air France: pp. 115, 170
John Taylor: p. 4
International News Photo: p. 27
Pere Jean-Marie: p. 32
Vie Catholique: p. 121
P. Almasy: p. 121
Jean-Pierre Landenberg: p. 125
Michel Simonet: p. 126
Editrice ELLE DI CI: p. 129
Black Star: pp. 130-134
Edouard Luntz: p. 136
Miller Service: p. 140
YAN: p. 142
J.-D. Lajoux: pp. 144-145
S. N. C. F.: p. 156
Photo C. I. R. I. C.: p. 169
Sansone: p. 172
CII-Claude Hermil: pp. 186-187
Wide World Photo: p. 188
Hove Camera Club, Brighton: p. 205
CSF: p. 209
Novalis: Front cover and p. ii

Originally published by Editions
du Chalet, Lyon, France, as
Audio-Visuel et Foi.

Book Design: Dan Johnson

Library of Congress Catalog
Card Number: 70-133407

Pflaum
38 West Fifth Street
Dayton, Ohio 45402

Published 1970

Printed in the United States of
America

contents

part one:

audio-visual
language
and faith

chapter 1:

mass media
and catechetics

PIERRE BABIN

tomorrow is today

Never before in history has society undergone a cultural revolution such as we are presently experiencing. The way we live, communicate and act is undergoing a fundamental change.

Yesterday: textbooks and blackboards;

Today: television and computerized teaching.

Yesterday: communication by letters and public speaking;

Today: tape recorders, telephones, records and films.

Yesterday: the little red schoolhouse;

Tomorrow: television programs originating from anywhere on the earth will be transmitted 24 hours a day via telecommunication satellites.

Yesterday: slow and indirect communication;

Tomorrow: to reach my friend in China, I will simply have to push a few buttons and then speak directly to him when he appears on the screen of my videophone.

TOMORROW? It seems incredible: video-tape recorders, teletypes, telecommunications.

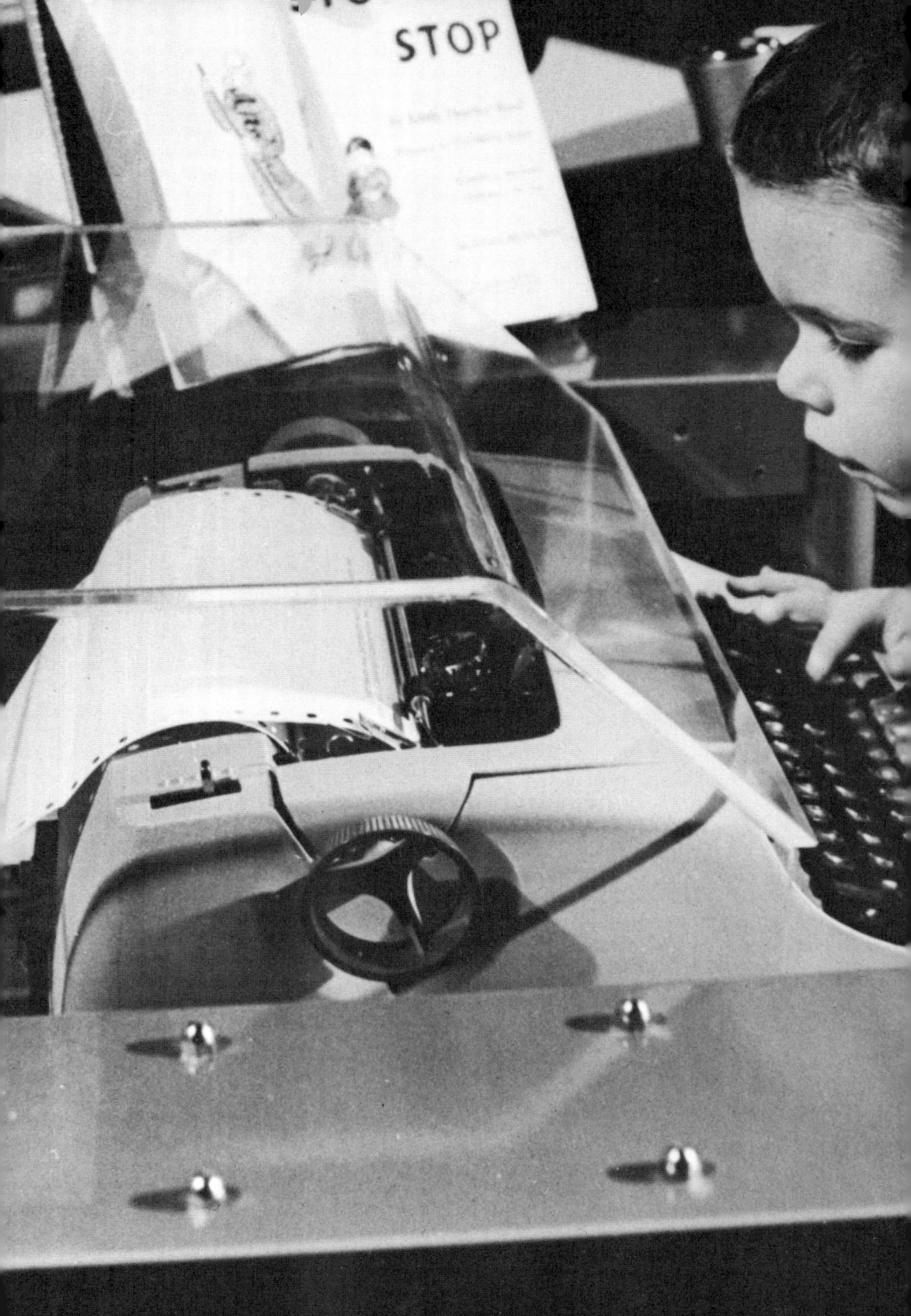

It is no exaggeration to speak of an unprecedented cultural transformation, of a "leap forward" for man and for mankind. This "leap forward" is not a dream; it is a fact, a fact resulting from scientific and technological progress.

WHAT IS CHANGING?

The organization of cities?

The architecture of houses?

The types of hobbies people have?

The assembly-line work in factories?

Yes, indeed.

But, above all,

Man is changing.

A new kind of man is being born.

7

It is interesting to see two children, one eight years old and the other five, watching a foreign cartoon with subtitles. The older child knows how to read while the younger does not. Strangely enough, it is the younger child who understands the movie better. Since he cannot read, his attention is focused upon the images. The older child feels he must read and understand the subtitles, and consequently misses many of the images. The preliterate child has a global and spontaneous understanding of the film, while the older child has only a fragmented and partial understanding.

This simple illustration is a revealing example of the new audio-visual man. Never before has man invented so much so rapidly. This rapid development makes it impossible to even imagine what tomorrow's world will be like. It is already evident that the mass media are rapidly turning our world into a "global village." Man has already broken the fetters that have bound him to earth, and is exploring the limitless possibilities of a whole new universe.

It is not only a question of a new universe and new inventions, but of a new kind of man, with a new way of communicating, of living and understanding, a new mental framework, a new kind of activity and involvement.

Already the traditional teaching methods have proven inept for children who have grown up with television.

For the last few years, much of the audio-visual research and literature has centered around the controversial ideas of Marshall McLuhan, a professor at the University of Toronto. McLuhan's penetrating analysis[1] of today's cultural transformation is not only concerned with new means of communication, but especially with a new type of person. When McLuhan says "The Medium is the Massage," he means that the new media of communication have formed or shaped a new type of person, with new patterns of learning. He is not primarily interested in audio-visual technology, but in the man it has produced. It is essential to understand this if audio-visuals are to be more than gimmicks used to attract young people's attention.

[1]Marshall McLuhan, *Understanding Media: the Extensions of Man* (New York: New American Library, 1964).

The real significance of audio-visual language in catechetics has often been misunderstood. For some time now audio-visual materials have been used in catechetical programs but often without any real knowledge or understanding of the technological revolution in mass communication. Catechists must become aware of the significance of this decisive event: a new man is being born, a man who learns and communicates in a new way, and who speaks a new language. Is it then still possible to go on "speaking of faith" in the same manner as before? What is the significance of the audio-visual revolution for catechetics?

There are three common misunderstandings regarding the use of audio-visuals in contemporary catechetics.

1 Most catechists today are aware of the force and power of mass media and think that these new resources should also be used in the spreading of the Gospel. They see the commercial use of mass media, its success in selling almost anything. Some even think that the mass media are responsible for influencing young people toward all sorts of delinquent behavior such as drug addiction and crime. "If mass media have so much influence for evil, why can they not be powerful means for good?" This kind of thinking leads the catechist to be more concerned with the audio-visual techniques than with the audio-visual man. Catechists find themselves searching for the most powerful means of dominating their students rather than of liberating them in the true spirit of the Gospel.

2 Audio-visuals are often used in catechetics as gimmicks. Films, records and tapes are ways of getting the student's attention. The catechist feels that once this attention is gained, he has a captive audience for "getting the message" across. In this case, audio-visuals are merely attention-gaining techniques and not an in-depth language for expressing the faith.

3 In practice, audio-visuals in catechetics have often been limited to the use of pictures. In the past, the auditory aspect of this new language has been neglected. Sound was often used in isolation rather than as a form of coexpression. This type of approach points out a common misunderstanding of young people's new patterns of learning. It is not a question of appealing to one sense after another, but of bringing about the multisensory experience that modern man requires.

the
real issue:
a new
kind
of man

The real issue: **a new kind of man who communicates in a new way.**

Man himself is undergoing a fundamental change. It is no longer possible to communicate with him unless we are taking this change seriously. It is not simply a question of methods and techniques, of adding a few pictures, records or films. It is above all **being a new kind of man:** this is the real issue.

Nor is it merely a question of novelty, but of fidelity to the Incarnation, of fidelity to man and to God. What is happening to a boy who reads 18,000 pages of comics a year, who is consistently listening to radio, records, looking at television, or going to movies? What new ways of learning, of understanding, and of being, has the multisensory experience of audio-visual language created? How must we change in order to reach adolescents who have been attuned to the latest TV commercials since they were four years old?

A DOUBLE INQUIRY

A true understanding of audio-visuals in catechetics does not lead us to a study of the technology of mass media but to a study of the man formed by mass media. This is the first area of investigation: What are the characteristic traits of audio-visual man? How does he grasp reality? How does he communicate? How does he learn? This will be dealt with in Chapter 2.

Once we have deepened our understanding of this new man, a further question must be asked: Can audio-visual language, the language of modern man, truly express the faith? Can it be an appropriate language for modern catechetics? For whom? At what age level? Under what conditions? These questions will be answered in Chapters 3 and 4.

It is only through this double inquiry that the real significance of the use of audio-visual language in catechetics can be understood. This, consequently, is the purpose of Part one.

In the remaining chapters, the "how" of using audio-visual materials in catechetics will be discussed.

This is just the beginning of the electronic era and we are still in the initial stages of inquiry.

What is important, however, is to have some understanding of the problem.

Our purpose, is to point out a few landmarks so that we can move further along new paths that man has begun to tread.

a new man is being born

chapter 2

audio-visual man

PIERRE BABIN

How does audio-visual amplification affect man? How does the TV generation grasp reality? What new type of man is emerging from recent technological developments?

These questions are dealt with by McLuhan in *The Gutenberg Galaxy*[1] and this present analysis owes much to his findings. Reading about audio-visual man, however, will not replace personal experience. Every educator can train himself to become aware of his own reactions to the audio-visual culture by allowing himself to be "massaged" by songs, TV programs and films. Then he can ask himself: What was happening to me during this experience? What was I becoming? Creative expression of oneself through photography, films and tapes will be helpful in measuring the influence of this new language.[2]

[1] Toronto: University of Toronto Press, 1962.

[2] For further development, see Chapter 8.

the birth
of a
new man

The wheel . . .

. . . is an extension of the foot.

The development of mass media through electronics has extended man's body and given him a new awareness of his senses. When you first drive a car, for example, you do not know the car, do not "feel" it, and therefore you drive carefully, afraid to pass or to be passed. Little by little, this fear disappears, allowing you to drive faster and faster. Gradually you become accustomed to the car. At the beginning, the car was just a strange object protecting you from the obstacles on the road, from the other cars. Gradually it became an extension of your body: the brakes and the accelerator became an extension of your foot; the fenders, an extension of the right and left sides of your body.

When the car rushed past an obstacle, it was as though your hips were being grazed.[3]

A new man is being born. McLuhan describes this new man in his book *The Medium is the Massage.*[4]

"All media are extensions of some human faculty—psychic or physical."[5]

The wheel is an extension of the foot; the phonetic alphabet is an extension of the eye; clothes are an extension of the skin; electronic media are extensions of the central nervous system.

[3]Psychologists have analyzed this same behavior in the way a baby relates to his body. In the first months of his life, a baby does not master the movements of his arms and legs. It is only through repeated exercises that his physical body becomes the instrument by which the world is communicated to him and he communicates himself to the world.

[4]New York: Bantam Books, 1967. The mass media (press, TV, radio) can be seen as massaging agents. McLuhan has used the association message-massage to show that the massage (the influence of the media) is more important than the message (the content expressed through the media).

Such is audio-visual man. The new media do not remain exterior to him. He cannot look at television without being involved. After a while, television, regardless of the content of the program, literally amplifies the eye and the ear, amplifies the need to see and hear as well as the way in which we see and hear.

Once the senses have been awakened by electronic media, in-depth involvement becomes as basic as the need to breathe. This explains why so many people keep their radio or TV on at all times. Modern man has acquired new dimensions. The extension of his body makes it difficult for him to adjust to experiences that are not all-inclusive sensory experiences.

TWO CONSEQUENCES:

a) When moralists rate films or television programs according to content only, they unknowingly draw attention away from the real issue. The moral problem of television is that it remains outside of the real self, that man is living with an extended body, without really being aware of it. If television is to be an extension of "my body," of my eyes and ears, I must know what I want to do with my body. I must know to what, and to whom, I want to give myself.

McLuhan has brought this out in the chapter "Challenge and Collapse":

Once we have surrendered our senses and nervous systems to the private manipulation of those who would try to benefit from taking a lease on our eyes and ears and nerves, we don't really have any rights left. Leasing our eyes and ears and nerves to commercial interests is like handing over the common speech to a private corporation, or like giving the earth's atmosphere to a company as a monopoly.[6]

[5]*Ibid,* page 26.

[6]Marshall McLuhan, *Understanding Media: the Extensions of Man* (New York: New American Library, 1964), page 73.

Is it not important that man has sold himself out so unknowingly?

Children are unconsciously starting to react to this situation: One fourteen-year old commented, "At night I can never talk with my parents. The TV is always on and if I say anything, someone points to the set and says, 'Keep quiet . . .' " "I go to my grandmother's," answered another, "because she doesn't have TV." Where does the real problem lie? The real problem lies not in the content but in the fact that parents have allowed their bodies to be extended in a more or less narcissistic manner: they now find themselves unable to communicate with their children, unable to express—through their extended bodies—their love and concern.

b) The second consequence is the influence of the medium on man. "The medium is the massage." What is important is not what is said on television but television itself. This has reshaped man and influenced him in depth. The message, the content, has only a secondary role. A man who always walks is a different person from the man who always drives.

The medium "makes" the man. When man extends his foot by means of the wheel, he becomes much more powerful, eager, and impatient.

It is also important to understand that these new extensions of man radically transform every sense ratio and restructure man's personality and values. The way an apartment is decorated reflects the person who lives in it and at the same time profoundly influences that person. The media both structure and reflect a person.

McLuhan in his chapter on "The Gadget Lover,"[7] quotes William Blake's "Jerusalem":

If Perceptive Organs vary,
Objects of Perception seem to
vary: if Perceptive Organs close,
their Objects seem to close also.

McLuhan explains:

To behold, use or perceive any extension of ourselves to technological form is necessarily to embrace it. To listen to radio or to read the printed page is to accept these extensions of ourselves into our personal system and to undergo the "closure" or displacement of perception that follows automatically. It is this continuous embrace of our own technology in daily use that puts us in the Narcissus role of subliminal awareness and numbness in relation to these images of ourselves. By continuously embracing technologies, we relate ourselves to them as servomechanisms. That is why we must, to use them at all, serve these objects, these extensions of ourselves, as gods or minor religions. An Indian is the servomechanism of his canoe, as the cowboy of his horse or the executive of his clock.

Physiologically, man in the normal use of technology (or his variously extended body) is perpetually modified by it and in turn finds ever new ways of modifying his technology. Man becomes, as it were, the sex organs of the machine world, as the bee of the plant world, enabling it to fecundate and to evolve ever new forms. The machine world reciprocates man's love by expediting his wishes and desires, namely, in providing him with wealth. One of the merits of motivation research has been the revelation of man's sex relation to the motorcar.[8]

---

[7]*Ibid.*, chapter 4, p. 55 ff.

[8]*Ibid.*, pp. 55-56.
McLuhan has given us insight into the "massage" experienced through electric and electronic media. But it is difficult to accept completely that the medium is the massage. Of course, there are people who are "addicted" to television, but there are growing numbers of persons who consciously choose their programs, and for whom the content is the fundamental criterion. There are also some producers who believe that the making of a film primarily involves having something to say and saying it forcefully.

Audio-visual man, then, extends his senses in a variety of ways, and these extensions bring about a radical change in his personality. Through them, a new man comes into being.

After three thousand years of explosion, by means of fragmentary and mechanical technologies, the Western world is imploding. During the mechanical ages we had extended our bodies in space. Today, after more than a century of electric technology, we have extended our central nervous system itself in a global embrace, abolishing both space and time as far as our planet is concerned. Rapidly, we approach the final phase of the extensions of man—the technological simulation of consciousness. . . .[9]

THE WESTERN WORLD IS "IMPLODING"

If 19th-century man wanted to know the world, he had to go out and discover it, he had to become an **ex-plorer.** If modern man wants to discover the world, he has only to push a button and sit back: television brings the sounds and mysteries of the world into every household.

Implosion means that man no longer has to go out to meet the universe; it is the world that comes to him. Man has become like the radar on the mountaintop. His nervous system is constantly invaded by the whole world. To try to stop this invasion would be suicide; you cannot escape your body. The electronically-induced technological extensions of man's central nervous system are enabling man— and dooming him — to incorporate within himself the whole of mankind.

Yesterday, the problem was to go out and discover. Now the problem is to survive this invasion of one's "home" by all the sounds, sights and noises which are bombarding every household, and upsetting every individual's psychic structure.

[9]*Ibid.,* page 19.

18

CONSEQUENCES:

a) Nowness and simultaneity.

The consequences of this implosion cannot be fully estimated as yet. We do know, however, that man's concept of time and space are undergoing an unprecedented change.[10] These categories are not disappearing, but they are being radically transformed. Tomorrow, businessmen will arrive in New York two clock hours earlier than the time of their departure from Paris. Mass media constantly expose contemporary man to all that is going on at the very moment it happens. He can be almost anywhere he chooses within a few short hours. This is still limited to the planet earth, but the first major steps have already been taken to include outer space.

When Negroes revolt in Mississippi, I am there, I see it happening. And so do the people in Tokyo, in Moscow. The same in-depth involvement resulting from the tactile power of television is shared by the whole of humanity, just as all radar units react everywhere to the same wavelengths. When listening to the on-the-spot report of the 1968 Democratic convention, people, whether in Los Angeles or Toronto, were suddenly transported to Chicago and found themselves taking sides.

b) Nowness, participation and responsibility

Why have social concern and involvement become so important today? The words are not new. But there is a new awareness of their significance. Involvement is a consequence of technological mutation. Previously, it was through the local time and space categories that one participated in the village. Today, participation has taken on not a new meaning but a new dimension. We are becoming aware that the whole world has changed into a village through electronic media. Man suddenly finds himself unable to live without a world-conscience and sense of responsibility. The reasons are not moral, but technological: the world is now at my doorstep, just as the village was before.

---

[10]Psychiatrists and philosophers have given new emphasis to the categories of time and space to classify the different types of psychoses.

*Electric speed in bringing all so-
cial and political functions together in a sudden implosion has
heightened human awareness of
responsibility to an intense degree. It is this implosive factor
that alters the position of the
Negro, the teen-ager, and some
other groups. They can no longer
be* **contained**, *in the political
sense of limited association.
They are now involved in our
lives, as we in theirs, thanks to
the electric media.*[11]

In a striking dialogue written for
A. Resnais' film, *Loin du Vietnam (Far from Vietnam)*, J. Sternberg describes the present-day
drama of contemporaneity and
world responsibility:

*You want to know something?
This is the first war in history
that everybody can watch at the
same time. Nobody ever saw a
war so close, all the time, at the
very moment it is happening. No
one can say: If I had known. . . .
Now, they know, they see. The
bombs make real corpses! The
bullets make real holes!*

*So what? Pity? Fear? It's all hap-
pening in a piece of furniture.
Not in Vietnam, not in someone's head, not in the street,
but in a piece of furniture. One
has the Vietnam war in his living room like Grandpa had the
Reichshoffen canon. "World-
wide News" . . . Do you know
the result of such news? . . .
"Not Vietnam again!"*[12]

"Not Vietnam again!" This last
sentence of Sternberg's text is
very significant. Indifference,
boredom and even annoyance
toward some of the themes presented through mass media are
more and more evident. The issue of growing responsibility
is an increasingly debatable one.
Have the mass media produced
greater responsibility or merely
indifference? The answer is by
no means a simple one.

The film *Medium Cool* dramat-
ically presents this new age of
awareness. The recurring words:
"The whole world's watching,
no one's doing anything about
it" spell the paradox of this new
age; awareness, indifference and
involvement coexist in audio-
visual man.

[11]McLuhan, *Understanding Media*,
p. 20.

[12]*Coup d'Oeil*, No. 12, p. 101ff.

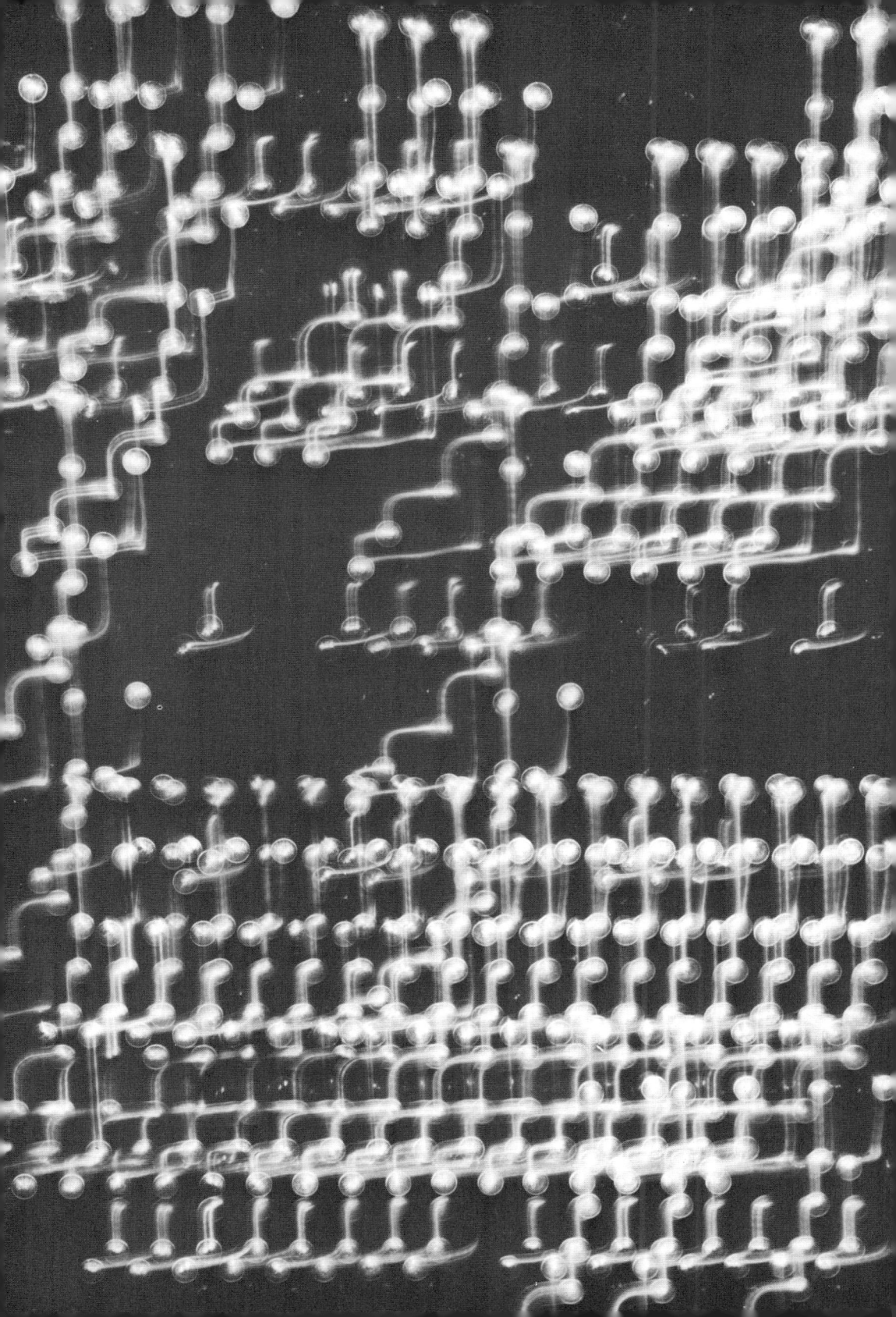

sensory man

How have mass media changed man's use of his senses?

Primarily it is the prevalence of a sensual and experiential grasp of reality over an intellectual and impersonal understanding of it.
For centuries, learning consisted essentially in reading books and listening to teachers. Today, audio-visual materials arousing in-depth involvement have replaced books and teachers. Reality instead of being filtered through writing and speech, is presented much more directly and powerfully with all the force of audio-visuals.

Previously the geography teacher would say: "The main products of Colombia are coffee and sugar cane." Today he brings Colombia into the classroom: "See, touch, notice the red colour of coffee when it is ripe and ready to be picked." The students find themselves in a pilot's seat, flying over the plantations, feeling the humidity and the hot sun on the coffee pickers' faces, seeing the luxurious vegetation and the never-ending rows of coffee plants. When the cameraman uses all the technical resources and potentialities of his media for visual and auditory amplification, the students unconsciously become eager, searching, anxious. They feel the heat as though they were actually right there.

a) Sensory man has new patterns of learning:
Just as a blind man learns by touching, so audio-visual man learns by in-depth involvement. He will understand through the effects that flashing neon signs, lavish displays, musical ads, radio and television have upon him. He understands primarily by direct contact and not by abstract representation. He is attuned to the connections between images, sensations, and sounds which render any intellectual explanation superfluous. He will actually think spontaneously with images and sounds.

This may be exemplified through the following contrast. Suppose two catechists are developing a research project on the personality of Jesus Christ: What type of man was he? The first point to be studied would be whether it is possible to really know someone. The educator brought up in a book-culture will search for comments of young people

It has been said of audio-visual man that he thinks with sounds and images, but there is more to it than that. This man sees with a camera, writes with a typewriter, hears through tape-recordings. In other words, the technical extensions must be included in any definition or appraisal of modern man's way of learning, understanding or doing. In order to learn, modern man needs the amplification and the sensory selection available to him through technology.

Primitive man was deeply involved in nature, and it appears that contemporary man is regaining this in-depth involvement and sensory participation. However, the sensory manner with which he became aware of reality is not the same for modern man as it was for primitive man. Primitive man was in direct contact with nature while modern man gets involved through the mediation of technical instruments. Watch a boy listening to a football game on his transistor, a family gathered around the television set, or a group of young people looking for subject matter for their next film. In each case, it is with technical media that the world is grasped and re-created. One of the most frequently employed symbols of modern man is the photographer, whether amateur or professional, who sees reality most clearly, understands and expresses it best, through the lenses of his camera.

and for excerpts from the writings of Carl Rogers, Rollo May, Abraham Maslow, Eric Erickson and others on the difficulty of knowing a person. The audio-visual educator, however, will try to remember the best auditory experiences, the best sounds which spell noncommunication to him—for example, a crowd of demonstrators being confronted by the police, or a passage from *2001: a Space Odyssey*. He can photograph one person in twenty different attitudes and ask: "Can any of these pictures reveal this person's **real-self**?"

Some people consider that audio-visuals give only impressions or superficial knowledge. The intelligent understanding upon which our culture has been built is rapidly disappearing, they will say. In reality, however, what is changing is only one form of intelligence and culture. The precision, exactness and quality of literary essays are now to be found in pictures and sounds, in audio-visual language, in I.B.M. machines and computers. These in their turn have become the most important nerve centers of this civilization.

Understanding reality through technology profoundly modifies perception and expression. Technology plays a threefold role: it filters, selects and amplifies. Consequently, to understand and express reality, technological instruments will exact of man a much more personal, active and recreative intervention. A photograph is not only a pictorial representation of nature, but nature as seen, selected and amplified by someone.

b) An overdeveloped sensory appetite:

Modern man has experienced an extraordinary sensory development. He needs sensory stimuli in order to start thinking, buying, working, communicating, praying . . . . Everywhere modern man creates for himself this type of environment: in large department stores we are confronted with music, light, pictures, colors, decorative gadgets, escalators and warmth. A similar atmosphere can be found wherever young people meet: records, guitars, dancing, lights, bright colors and iridescent posters.

Contemporary popular songs and modern music are generally much more sensuous than intellectual or spiritual experiences. Modern music has a visceral quality: when a singer like Tom Jones takes the microphone, no one remains indifferent. His gyrations, the tension of his voice create a very powerful effect. The whole audience gets involved in the act. Even their heartbeat and breathing seem to follow the nervous rapid rhythm of the singer.

After hearing a concert of percussion music, a group of adults and young people were discussing their reactions: "It is a very special type of music, quite superficial. It doesn't make me react much," commented one adult. "Maybe it affects you that way," replied a teenager, "but not me. I think this music is out of this world! It makes me feel as though I'm penetrating into the whole of the universe. Even ordinary, everyday experiences take on a wonderful, poetic dimension." In this conversation, the gap is easily seen: one is living a rich sensory experience unknown to the other.

There is still another facet to audio-visual man which gives rise to a delicate and complex problem. Although mass media are no longer considered anti-intellectual,[13] they nevertheless tend to produce lethargy in a great number of people. Why is this?

[13]See Edgar Morin, l'Esprit du Temps, Paris (ed. Grasset).

The October 1968 issue of Documents-Service-Adolescence presented a survey of 1300 students between the ages of 16 and 18, from 23 different schools in Versailles; all of these students were from TV-owning homes. The survey revealed that 880 organized their life according to TV; 1081 chose their programs because of content; 862 discussed the program with their parents, 851 with their friends; 666 were able to give reasons for and against TV. Is this passivity?

. . . the psychology of learning demonstrates that the senses of sight and hearing account for 94% of all learning. Furthermore, an in-depth study by Mobil Oil Company of all income groups of both white and blue collar workers showed that after three days only 10% of the material taught by simple telling could be recalled, 20% of the material was recalled which had been only shown, while 65% of the material taught by both telling and showing was recalled.[16]

Physiologically, the studies of Hans Selye on the state of shock indicate that one of the body's first reactions to extreme stress can be numbness.[14] For example, the carpenter who cuts his finger on an electric saw feels nothing for an instant. The central nervous system protects itself by isolating the "overstimulated" organ. Something similar takes place in man when he is brutally invaded by today's mass media. Everyday experience seems to strengthen this hypothesis. Middle-aged people, for instance, are much more passive than young people when watching films or television. Because their nerves are less accustomed to the audio-visual invasion, they react with numbness or indifference. Young people's senses are more alert and they react to the media with greater interest and personal involvement.[15]

What conclusions can be drawn regarding audio-visual man? Experimental studies confirm not only the existence of sensory intelligence, but also its importance in the act of learning:

Although very little scientific data is yet available, it seems obvious that the intellectual development of a 17th - century man is not the same as that of a 20th-century audio-visual man. Certainly his mind functions differently. However, there is no reason to believe that he will be less human, less free and creative, less capable of understanding and of believing.

From a certain point of view, what is the effect of mass media's powerful influence on contemporary man?

---

[14]See H. Selye, *The Stress of Life* (New York: McGraw-Hill, 1956.)

[15]Because of the practical orientation of this book, little more will be said on these critical issues. This is not meant to minimize their importance but to stay within the range of pedagogy. For further reading, see Chapter 4 of McLuhan's *Understanding Media.*

[16]Emery Tang, "Understanding the listener as a movie-goer," in *Preaching*, vol. 2, no. 5 (September-October, 1967), p. 28.

Commercial audio-visual dealers know the process is inevitable: the customer who buys black and white television will be back before long for a color set; someone who has learned to appreciate a good record player will soon want something better than his $39.95 deal.

Man has to free himself from the sensual slavery that can result from constantly craving deeper and more powerful sensory pleasures.[17] Yet this driving force is also part of man's effort to grow. Better sounds, better pictures, better contrasts are part of that never-ending search to experience life more fully.

Traditional asceticism distrusts sensory man. Certainly, to abstain, to choose, and to refuse will always be part of life. But would it not be infidelity to the Word of Life to sacrifice the senses that ought to help man live more fully? Asceticism should not repress the senses, but develop them qualitatively. Highly developed senses are needed in order to live Psalm 150 which enjoins man to praise the Lord with his whole being and with everything that affects his life.

The Christian should have a positive attitude towards the mass media, for through them he can rediscover the creative power of the senses. This awakening makes greater faith and love possible in the true spirit of the Gospel. Through his senses man touches reality, and this reality enables him to discover the One in whom "we live and move and have our being" (Acts 17: 28, RSV).

---

[17]Slavery is understood here in the psychological rather than the moral sense. There is slavery when overdeveloped and stimulated senses are not directed by the spirit. A slave is one whose sensual pleasure is not directed to a better communion with others.

a new type of intelligence

It is difficult to describe audio-visual man's understanding. The fact that the audio-visual factor is not the only one that contributes to intellectual development only renders the task more difficult.

The first change brought about that can be observed is somewhat negative. This new civilization tends to eliminate the literary, intellectual, reflective abstract and conceptual type. The events of May, 1968, in France, for example, mark the birth of a new language; young people were challenging the old gods of the Sorbonne.

But where are we going?

In response to this question, two complimentary images may be proposed: the electronic computer and the human eye. The first speaks of intelligence as the ororganizing power, the second speaks of intelligence as intuitive and symbolical.

The calculating mind?

Modern man is invaded by a mosaic of impressions, pictures and perspectives. How does he go about understanding these? Audio-visual man does not try to reason and reflect, but begins by organizing the various facts and information coming in from all sides. He does this rapidly and in a global manner. He establishes connections, links between pictures and sounds, between foreground and background, between the man who is sleeping and this other man who is walking slowly toward him. Everything goes so fast, so many things come up at the same time, that understanding can only mean making a maximum of connections. Selecting and analyzing one particular point has become impossible. What does understanding mean for a man who reads *Life, Time* or the local newspaper, while taking the train home at night? He is not trying to penetrate, to go deeply and thoroughly into what he is reading. He merely wants to know the general trend of international and local events, to "be in the know," to participate.

But what does seeing and understanding mean in relation to pictures, for instance?

It means distinguishing the essential from the secondary aspects. It means sorting subject from context, the factual from the emotional dimension.

It also means understanding the visual symbols: all that in the written text is called grammar and syntax:

. . . *Coexpression, though still young, is the language of twentieth century communications, a language dependent on two senses, two styles, two sensibilities—and creating a new sense of information, a new way of reaching another, a fresh way of thinking . . .*

. . . *When an image and words can coalesce to form a fresh kind of language—demanding an interplay between words and image, and between the word-image combination and the reader or viewer—then coexpression has happened. The interplay, a key selling factor in many ads or commercials and one of the mainstays of comics, makes coexpression more complex than pure words in its mode of involvement, and hence capable of creating a wider range of responses.*[18]

It becomes evident that in this regard the mind of audio-visual man closely resembles an IBM computer: its function is to translate, sort, compare, organize, read, give the answer in a minimum of time. One business manager, reflecting upon his experience, acknowledged: "I feel like an IBM machine. . . . All day long I receive a mass of information, signals, problems that must be immediately solved. That's what my morning mail is all about. Sometimes I don't know what to say; it's as though my 'machine' were overworked, or didn't have sufficient information and time to calculate and correlate everything. The only solution is to wait until things clear up, and I find the missing link. . . ."

Missing link: this expression is very significant. Reasoning seems to follow a new pattern; its logic works with information, signals and sensory impulses, connecting them in such a way as to bring about understanding and decisions.

---

[18]William Kuhns and Robert Stanley, "Coexpression and religious language," in *The Religious Situation: 1969*, edited by Donald R. Cutler (Boston: Beacon Press, 1969), pp. 869, 871.

The eye:

The obvious objection, of course, is that an IBM machine does not have human intelligence. Consequently our second image, the eye, can be helpful here. These two aspects of audio - visual man's learning process are intricately interwoven to make up his "human" understanding. The eye is intuition—that is, the capacity to grasp the meaning of things immediately, and thus to give a certain orientation and patterning to sensory impressions and information. Intuition includes both a contact with reality and a withdrawal from it that results in an intelligent pattern. Intuition is seeing goals; it is a global understanding of problems that must be solved, of values that must be reached, of dimensions that must be emphasized. All of these are specifically human capabilities, beyond the scope of any machine.

This type of symbolic and intuitive intelligence seems to characterize many young people engaged in scientific and technical training. Is the new sensory development promoting a greater spiritual sensitivity, a greater symbolic awareness? Or is it simply the idealism of youth? It is too soon to know. However it is evident that young people today, in the scientific disciplines, are a curious blend of rigor and sensitivity, of pragmatism and awareness of people, of efficiency together with a gen-

uine need for human relationships. For most classical intellectuals, this constitutes a paradox that is difficult to understand. A frequent cause of unrest among university students has been the emphasis upon science and technology to the neglect of the humanities. And this unrest has been evident even among those engaged in the scientific and technical disciplines. These students rebel against a scientific approach which fails to be humanitarian in its objectives.

Audio-visual man with his new type of intelligence has not yet been fully analyzed. He seems to have a propensity to participate, linking intelligence and life, understanding and practical action. For audio-visual man, understanding is above all sensitivity to and participation in the rhythm of this world. It is to be "in" and "with," grasping reality not only through intellectual understanding, but through a vital contact with reality itself. Reflection and critical thinking are being increasingly replaced by a need to participate, a yearning for action that can transform or at least better the human condition. Abstract reasoning, formal thinking and literary precision are giving way to more spontaneous and creative expression.

This description of audio-visual man cannot be presented as a final analysis, supported by statistical proofs; these are not yet available to us. The reader must verify the accuracy of this description by means of his own experience.

ing and beautiful." But not everyone reacts in this way. "I'm really afraid audio-visuals will destroy the purity and clarity of our faith," one priest commented. "Nothing is as ambiguous as pictures and music! You can make a picture say anything you want." Another added: "Faith is communicated only through interpersonal dialogue. Films, slides and records can never be a substitute for personal contact."

chapter 3:

is audio-visual language apt to express faith?

PIERRE BABIN

Can A-V language express faith? Theoretically, the answer to this question should be simple, but in reality, it is often complex and debatable. For example, two students had just viewed a good catechetical montage.[1] "If that's what religion is, I'm interested," one says. "Professions of faith, definitions, theories, all those abstract ideas are useless. I've had enough of them!" "That goes for me too," the other replied. "This gets you thinking and gives you something concrete to talk about. You get the impression you are involved in something interest-

Is audio-visual language, then, really apt to express faith? This question must be answered with more than a general theory about the necessity of using audio-visual media. In an effort to deal with this question, several people who are actually using this language in catechesis were interviewed. We realize, of course, that there are still very few people who have acquired the necessary competency in this field, and that their experience has yet to stand the test of time. Every educator, however, can compare their experience with his own. Our objective is not to establish a definitive thesis, but rather to make catechists more sensitive to the issues involved in the use of audio-visuals in catechetics. A certain amount of overlapping is unavoidable, but we will try to bring out the major advantages and risks which have become evident through experimentation.

[1]The word "montage" here refers to a series of slides or pictures with a corresponding sound-track which may include music, text, and sound effects.

"Only that which is suggested
can be called poetic."
—H. Bremond

advantages

1. Audio-visuals evoke more than they define.

A group of 14-15-year-old students from a boys' Catholic high school had agreed to meet with students of the same age from a girls' school in order to discuss how boys and girls their age see each other. At the beginning of the session they were all uncomfortable about how to start the discussion until one of the girls said: "I'd like to project a slide I took downtown, except that maybe I shouldn't. . . . It's the hosiery advertisement that's plastered all over town—a close-up of a girl's leg as she puts on her stocking. I think it's degrading. Why do men see us this way?" She projected the slide and then asked the boys: "Is this the way you see us?" The concrete picture and the straightforward question opened up the discussion immediately.

Mass media suggest rather than explain. They go beyond illustrations and move one to discover a deeper meaning in things. A student who saw the movie *Cool Hand Luke* several times remarked, "I like to see Christ in that way." This film is hardly a catechetical definition of Christ, but the atmosphere and situation suggest the mystery of man's relationships with God.[2]

[2]In this context, Bernard Favrel emphasizes the need and the value of a language to express faith that comes from an unconscious organization of language: "Could pictures liberate us from our need of 'looking under every branch', this artificial search for applications of our faith, for over-precise projections of how we should grow; from having to establish cross-walks between faith and our sense world. An imagery that remains open, that is relatively imprecise because it has so many possibilities, that is unstructured and yet to which we can often return—such an imagery can 'accompany' growth in faith with more authenticity and accuracy than the overly precise formulations of the conscious intellectual mind." (*Reflects Cate-Club* Dec. '68, p. 5)

2. Audio-visuals help to develop an emotional response to reality.

Films and montages that are apt to express spiritual values seem to work in two ways:

a) they make us think

b) they involve us emotionally in the situation

"It really makes you wonder about life!" young people will say. This is their way of expressing man's basic need to find something beyond the material reality of things. This communion with the beyond includes both a search and a sense of peace; a question as well as an answer. When Jesus first began gathering disciples about him, he did not say, "Come and attend my lectures!" but rather, "Come and see!" In other words—learning by participation. A "good" audio-visual montage on Abraham, for example, will not be one that illustrates his travels with extensive historical references, but one that awakens in the viewer an aspiration for that "land beyond," and arouses in him a need to search for "something more." Here again the knowledge resulting from such a catechesis will not be conceptual or intellectual, but symbolic.

3. Audio-visuals encourage creativity.

People who have been initiated into the use of audio-visuals in catechetics experience the joy of creativity. This "need to be creative" is a slogan frequently heard today among young people, and particularly among students. It seems to reveal their need to break down those closed systems in which the world is well organized and logical, in order to find new ways of expressing man's deepest needs and instincts.

Experience seems to confirm that as soon as young people learn to express their faith in color, sound, music, or the plastic arts, their faith ceases to be passive and static. Rather than resorting to speculative thinking, they begin exploring to discover new dimensions, new horizons, new meanings in the world around them. It is as though they had suddenly learned to speak a new language.

Experience also confirms that working with photos helps young people to be more expressive and allows free association of ideas. There is a tremendous difference between a group that uses photos to communicate and one in which expression is limited to the oral communication of ideas, attitudes, and feelings.

Where will such creativity lead us? Audio-visuals will definitely break through traditional catechetical formulas. They will require a new kind of faith that is more comfortable with creativity and research than with ready-made syntheses, because they immerse us in the world of the senses. Sensory experience and the awakening of basic instincts are always at the source of new movements and great periods of creativity. Through audio-visuals, the mind is rediscovering the body. When we thus recognize that man is more than intellect, we become more fully ourselves, and we react to reality not only with our mind but with our feelings and emotions as well.

4. Audio-visuals foster personal involvement.

Air France posters by Matthieu, advertising foreign countries elicit a strong reaction from young people.

There is no color and yet it seems to be alive.

This is clearly what is most typical of audio-visual language.

It gets you involved. It stirs an emotional response.

It makes you want to do something.

"It really makes me feel like going to that country!"

"Fiestas, carnivals, anguish, joy, and excitement all at once . . ."

"A whirlwind—that's my problem too!"

"I saw the film *Parable*[3] and the next day I felt like a different person," a student commented. "I had learned something about the Gospel that really changed my outlook. The pictures of racism and of man's inhumanity to man kept running through my mind while I kept repeating: 'One day a man came who dared to be different.' "

This reaction seems to be typical of many young people who saw the movie and illustrates the new kind of faith-response which audio-visual language fosters. It gives us a new view of life that invites us to grow through personal involvement rather than abstract formulas and behavior codes. The student's further comment: "I couldn't forget the clown—his eyes, his way of acting, his way of reacting to false attitudes" indicates the direction in which the person viewing the film wants to grow.

5. Audio-visuals help to develop critical awareness.

Art develops a critical awareness towards culture and civilization.

In the words of Marcuse:

The rupture with (the societal reality), the rational transgression, is an essential quality of even the most affirmative art; it is alienated also from the very public to which it is addressed. No matter how close and familiar the temple or cathedral were to the people who lived around them, they remained in terrifying or elevating contrast to the daily life of the slave, the peasant and the artisan—and perhaps even to that of their masters.

---

[3]*Parable* (16mm film; 22 min.). Produced by Fred Wiles Inc. for the Protestant Council of Churches, New York City, 1964. Distributed by Mass Media Ministries, 1714 Stockton Street, San Francisco 94133, U.S.A.

Whether ritualized or not, art contains the rationality of nega-tion. In its advanced positions, it is the Great Refusal—the protest against that which is.[4]

While audio-visuals cannot be identified with art, they never-theless seem to have more affin-ity with art than with written or oral language. In order for their sensory appeal and inherent am-biguity to be effective, audio-vis-uals must have artistic quality. Films certainly require greater artistic and poetic talent than a casual conversation or even a university lecture.

Only to the extent that audio-visuals have such artistic quality will they transcend banality and mediocrity. They help us to take a new look at the world, as well as at life itself. Artists who insist on "art for art's sake" tend to limit audio-visuals to self-ex-pression and consequently have little impact on the general pub-lic. Nevertheless, these artists do remind us of our need for a world more beautiful than the one in which we are living, and of the necessity of a radical re-fusal of the "status quo."[5] With-out going to extremes, we should recognize that audio-visual lan-guage fosters a freedom of ex-pression, a greater need to be creative, and a sensitivity to beauty that make people dis-satisfied with the mediocrity and drabness that are built into our society. As soon as young people become involved with contem-porary language, they become more sensitive to sound, rhythm, and color, as well as to the world in general and their role in it. Although the psychedelic character of young people's self-expression may irritate adults, these same psychedelic patterns express an aspiration for a better world as well as what Marcuse calls "the Great Refusal" of me-diocrity in traditional life styles.

---

[4]Herbert Marcuse, *One-Dimen-sional Man* (Boston: Beacon Press, 1964), p. 63.

[5]The relationship between art and audio-visuals is a problematic one. It is very important to maintain the aesthetic requirements of audio-visual media, but it is also important to relativize the aesthe-tic criteria in catechetical audio-visuals. When addressing a group of scholars, the speaker must be very careful about the quality and correctness of his language. When speaking to a group of young people, repetition, and minor gram-matical errors may be aids to com-munication. This applies to audio-visual catecheses: if they are for the general public, their quality need not be the kind required for a film club. The primary criterion of audio-visual language is that it communicate.

risks

A great deal of subjectivity is involved in developing creativity, participation, affectivity, and critical awareness. Any approach that relies to such a degree on subjective elements inevitably involves risks. Two main areas of concern will be analyzed here:

1. Lack of clarity and precision

2. Lack of structure and synthesis

1. Lack of clarity and precision

In a public audience held on October 30th, 1968, Paul VI stated: "Thinking is neglected in our image-oriented civilization."[6] Clearly, however, the audio-visual era is not only an era of pictures. Audio-visual language does communicate knowledge that is less precise than book knowledge and the spoken word. A formula is more precise than a series of pictures, sounds, and poetic words. Nevertheless, thought as such has not disappeared. On the contrary, many people assert that a film or a montage has made them do a great deal more thinking than any sermon or oral catechesis. A certain kind of thinking is losing ground: **thinking that stresses precise ideas, exact wording, and rigorous logic.**

Young people today prefer evocative and symbolic language to precise formulations of faith.[7] This preference makes them at home with the new language of audio-visuals.

In this respect our era is highly paradoxical. We seem to be experiencing a gradual separation between the extremely rigorous and objective language of computers and audio-visual language which seeks to communicate experience, emotion, and meaning, as well as factual information.

This creates problems for the expression of faith. While the rediscovery of symbolic and evocative language is an enrichment, nevertheless it would be unfortunate if we were to abandon clear and accurate language completely. This could endanger the expression of our faith, particularly in this age of scientific precision.

---

[6] See L'Osservatore Romano, October 31, 1968.

[7] The two kinds of language are studied in J. Colomb's Le Service de l'Evangile, Vol. I, pp. 470-500. The author has a fine philosophical and catechetical analysis of the relationship between symbolical thought and rational thought, their diversity and their unity.

2. Lack of structure and synthesis

This second risk is in some ways very similar to the first. In a recent catechetical institute, two groups were easily distinguishable: those who preferred working with peers in a team and those who preferred lecture-type courses. The first group explained: "We have to learn to question, to share ideas, to discover by ourselves!" whereas the second replied: "But we have no overview, no background information with which to work. We're wasting our time."

This contrast is difficult to cope with and can only be solved through some form of compromise. We might say that the first group were "McLuhanites" whereas the second belonged to the "Gutenberg Galaxy."[8] The former said: "Why worry about a synthesis? It's probably going to change completely in three years anyway. Dialogue is what we need, learning how to bring together different viewpoints in order to gain a more valid vision of the world and to respond to it more effectively." Two different types of knowledge are involved here: lineal and mosaic. The first group supported its point by referring to McLuhan's thesis that mosaic knowledge gives openness, a sense of direction, constant questioning, and an ability to establish connections rapidly.[9]

We can sense here the transformation that is taking place. The lineal man, the man with the logic and the discursive syllogisms, relates to the world in terms of a highly - structured worldview and logical correlations. The audio-visual man, however, relates to the world through his skills in communication and his experience of meaning, rather than through a set of principles and categories. This, of course, demands a different kind of faith-life and a new kind of Christian. We are leaving behind us that age of Christianity typified by the products of Catholic liberal arts colleges and entering an age typified by such men as John F. Kennedy. This new kind of man draws his strength not so much from an overall intellectual synthesis of life and of the world, as from a general thrust of spirit that becomes more precise through constant searching and questioning within a community context.

This new style of Christian life definitely involves risks, particularly the lack of definite structures and a clear vision of things.

---

[8]This is perhaps an oversimplification of the problem, but one which serves to bring out the central issues. Certainly other factors can lead us to prefer a lecture-type approach—for example, the opportunity to hear a leading authority or to obtain a synthesis of someone's thinking.

[9]Marshall McLuhan, *The Gutenberg Galaxy* (Toronto: University of Toronto Press, 1968), p. 265 ff.

43

Christians today are experiencing the pain of the collapse of structures. The traditional ideological strength has disappeared. We are beginning an age of pluralism in which everyone must remake his synthesis every day, and must learn to discern the difference between the real and the transient. The following excerpt from a letter describes the storm center of such a crisis:

When we were young, we received a solid religious education. One of my uncles was a priest in a very poor parish in Waterbury, Connecticut, and I spent several summers with him. My father used to read a great deal of classical and religious literature. He had a beautiful philosophy that covered everything in life and in religion. His vision established deep roots in our minds.

Life was so simple then. There was just good and evil—no deviation. And we didn't look for excuses when we grew up and did foolish things. We knew when we were wrong.

Now it's like in poetry and in art. Everyone interprets things in his own way. It's all in the eye of the beholder. Perhaps that's the way it should be, but I don't like it. You hate to lose your fairy godmother and find yourself exposed to the naked truth. What is the naked truth? Maybe this is how the new generation understands it. I don't understand.

. . . Peter, pray for me.[10]

---

[10]Translated from Missi (Lyon, 12, Rue Sala), November 1968, p. 291.

option

Having discussed the use of audio-visuals in general, let us now consider their capacity for expressing the realities of faith. We believe they are most suitable, particularly in catechesis for adolescents, but only under certain conditions.

Why recommend audio-visuals?

If catechesis is understood as the first general proclamation of the faith,[11] then audio-visual language would appear eminently suitable, since it has the characteristic qualities required for such a initiation. It tends to provoke a reaction, to suggest symbolic meaning, to encourage further research, and it stimulates a desire to understand and transform reality. Theology, on the other hand, requires a structure and a precision that are less compatible with ambiguity inherent in audio-visual language.

Research has revealed that audio-visual language is more adapted to preschoolers, adolescents, and young people, than to children of the 9-12 age level or to adults. We need only compare a few of the traits characteristic of audio-visual language with those of youth and early childhood to understand why this is the case.

---

[11]J. Colomb, *Le service de l'Evangile*, Vol. 1 (Paris: Desclee) pp. 3-15.

Early Childhood, Adolescence, Youth.

—Period of predominance of the senses, of symbolic understanding, and of an emotional response to reality.

—Power of the imagination and importance of emotional factors in the learning process.

—Importance of the environmental atmosphere and of psychological identification in the learning process.

—Sensitivity to meaning and goals rather than to practical details.

—Pantheism, sensitivity to nature.[12]

Audio-visuals

—Auditory and visual amplification of the meaning given to reality.

—Importance of the atmosphere of sound and visual space.

—Impact on the senses and emotions.

—Invitation to in-depth involvement with nature or the environment. Extension of man to his environment by making him react and communicate rather than ponder within himself in an abstract way.

Although we are all to some extent immersed in this new language, these characteristics seem to make it particularly suitable for little children, teenagers, and young adults.

the use of audio-visual langauge in catechetics

1. **Audio-visual language must be a medium for communication.**

Audio-visuals should awaken and foster interpersonal relationships within the group. If they do not promote relationships then they are of no use, since Revelation can take place only where there is personal interaction among the people concerned.

---

[12]For further reading on these points, see J. Piaget, *Mechanisms of Perception* (New York: Basic Books, 1969), and *Psychology of Intelligence* (New York: Littlefield, 1968).

The following incident illustrates this point. An experienced missionary had been invited to speak to a large group of young people in order to promote interest in the missions. Instead of speaking directly to the audience, the missionary played a previously prepared tape-recording which expressed the message he wished to communicate to those present. While the audience was listening to the tape, the missionary went out for a smoke. The tape was excellent yet the audience was disappointed and angry. They resented the fact that the missionary had cut himself off from the group. Audio-visual media cannot replace the teacher, but should assist him in establishing personal relationships within the group.

Herein lies the greatest difficulty in the use of audio-visuals in catechesis. Many educators have great difficulty in relating freely with young people. Audio-visuals can easily become an unconscious shield against the students' questions and reactions. They tend to reinforce the barrier between the educator and the students. A catechist may start his class with a popular song or a film in order to avoid speaking to the students. The group may seem very interested but this interest is superficial. If there is no "sharing" in the class, there can be no "Revelation."

Audio-visuals require a greater personal involvement on the part of the educator than the traditional approach to catechesis, in the sense of a more democratic relationship between students and catechist. We must not use the media as instruments for domination but as means for establishing interpersonal relationships. They are a kind of universal language through which everyone can express himself in form, color, and sound.

Personal involvement has always been an essential part of any catechesis, but today, in our audio-visual civilization, this involvement must become stronger, binding students and catechist together. Ideally, audio-visuals should be used to promote discussion and relationships, to help people express themselves better, and to encourage research and creativity in the group.

Some people are beginning to realize that audio-visuals are bringing about a very important change, not only in catechetical methods but in the very life of the Church itself. They are creating a new type of human relationship and interpersonal communication. Right and wrong will no longer be so clear-cut; formulas of faith will be less dogmatic and intellectual syntheses will be less structured.

Many people find this very disturbing. Like Saint Augustine who feared that Christianity might disappear with the coming of the Barbarians, these people fear that so little emphasis on the intellectual expression of faith will mean the end of Christianity. This fear can be healthy if it makes us more aware of what's happening and helps us to safeguard the essentials in a changing world. But it must not paralyze us if our faith is to remain dynamic. We must adopt a new approach in order to maintain fundamental values beyond changing formulations. Catechetical audio-visuals will be effective if they help the individual live more fully and relate more authentically within the group. They will serve their purpose only if catechesis itself leads once more to "the sharing of the bread." The strength provided by the precision and highly structured quality of traditional catechesis can be found today in the quality of fraternal love and communication that exists within the group and which opens it to the constant guidance of the Holy Spirit.[13] You don't pour new wine into old wine-skins. (See Matt. 9-17)

2. Audio-visuals must promote liberty.

There is a real danger that with audio-visual language, rigid dogmatic formulas will be replaced by narcissistic contemplation through images and sounds. This would hardly be progress!

Audio-visual language has its own laws and its own rules of grammar. The catechist's task is not simply to master this language, but to do so in order to liberate men. Catechesis is intended to liberate people spiritually and to share with them our hope for a better world. Any catechetical interest in audio-visuals has to be justified by the need to liberate people and not simply to help the catechetical "pill" go down.

A Christian sees man's greatest liberation in Jesus Christ. Audio-visuals must not then be used simply as gimmicks to attract attention, but as a privileged language for proclaiming the "Good News" of Jesus Christ for modern man.

There are two specific dangers that must be carefully avoided in catechetics:

---

[13]For further development of this theme, see P. Babin, *Options* (New York: Herder and Herder, 1967, chapters 6 and 7).

a.) A self-centered use of audio-visuals

A catechist who really likes records, pictures, or films may often be seeking only himself in his use of media. He looks for himself in the songs, the films, or the photos he chooses. Instead of proclaiming the Good News of the Gospel, he is using the media to speak of himself. Instead of communicating the fullness of Christ's life, he projects his own self-image. Narcissism is an ever-present danger. McLuhan calls it the most serious danger.[14]

b.) The use of audio-visuals as a means of domination

Audio-visuals can also be a means of exercising power and of dominating others. Publicity and the use of television in political campaigns illustrate how the media can influence people. This abuse of audio-visuals has caused students in many countries to protest against the mass media.

Is it necessary to stress that the mass media — particularly the press, radio and television have become the principal targets of young people's anger? In July 1967, the young people of West Berlin denounced the "Springer" press as responsible for the intolerable situations that existed there. In Berkley, the first signs of the students' revolt were demonstrations against a segregationist newspaper. In Spain, students set fire to the newspapers

suspected of not describing the situation as it really was. In France, as early as May 1968, students demonstrated against the press, and in Paris they even considered attacking the Radio Center. Although this project was not carried out, it carried a great deal of weight in the journalists' decision to join the strikers and provide better information.[15]

3. Audio-visuals are no substitute for personal contact.

It has already been pointed out that contemporary audio-visuals are not exclusive, but inclusive. They do not suppress, they amplify. They do not dehumanize, but rather through them the sounds and sights of nature become part of man.

In reviewing such films as *2001, a Space Odyssey* and *Les Gauloises Bleues*, critics have written: "This film is a coded message that we cannot understand

---

[14]McLuhan, *Understanding Media*, pp. 51-56.

[15]*Presse-Actualite* (Paris, November, 1968), p. 10.

49

until we realize that we have understood everything but not with our intelligence: it is with another sense that movies are now revealing to us and that has nothing whatsoever to do with discursive reason."[16] This must be correctly understood: we are witnessing the end of a certain kind of literature, but not of words. On the contrary, the most concrete contemporary music makes extensive use of words.

Catechists using audio-visual language must avoid overemphasis upon pictures alone to the neglect of verbal communication. Film clubs provide valuable criteria for the use of audio-visuals in catechetics, but their too often exclusively pictorial emphasis must in no way restrict catechetical language. Radio and television are perhaps even more helpful in this regard because they use the everyday language of ordinary people. The importance of the spoken word must in no way be underestimated.

Similarly, audio-visuals and personal contact are mutually complementary and enriching rather than competitive techniques. Audio-visuals, as we have seen, promote interpersonal communication and can only be properly understood through personal discussion and exchange.[17] A film such as Parable, for instance, which uses very little dialogue, requires a good deal of discussion in order to be meaningful.

4. Poetic and artistic quality are essential.

The most important criteria for the use of audio-visuals in catechesis is their ability to promote spiritual reflection and communication. A picture is not catechetically good simply because it is aesthetically beautiful (a very subjective criteria) but because experience confirms that it arouses a "spiritual reaction" in people.

---

[16]See C. Mauriac, in l'Observateur (Paris, October 1, 1968), pp. 36-37.

[17]R. Barthes writes, "There is a dead-end in writing and it is precisely the dead-end of society itself. Writers today can feel it. For them, the search for an oral non-style, for a zero point or the point where writing and talking meet is the anticipation of an absolutely homogeneous state of society. Most of them know that there cannot be a universal language outside of a concrete universality of nations, other than a mystical or nominal one." ("L'audio-visuel, language nouveau," in Le Monde (Paris, September 29-30, 1968). p. 20.

This, however, does not eliminate the importance of artistic quality as one of the criteria by which to "judge" the value of audio-visual language. Certainly the masterpieces that have impact on mankind are great in terms of poetry and symbolism. Audio-visuals, it seems, create the spiritual reaction necessary in catechetics inasmuch as they appeal through symbolism to what is most profound in man. The artistic qualities in such films as *A Man for all Seasons* arouse a personal response within us.

When one appeals to what is deepest and ultimate in man, there is in fact a religious reaction. This "reaction" is not faith, but it is a psychological condition that opens one to the transcendent. The artistic quality of a work gives it the power to confront man and to provoke a spiritual reaction. While the aesthetic element is not the only criteria for catechetical audio-visuals, it is nevertheless an essential one.

5. Need for prophets.

"Rather than a church that indocrinates, we must become a Church that confesses Jesus Christ," said Msgr. Schmitt in addressing the Assembly of French Bishops at Lourdes in 1968. Audio-visual civilization, audio-visual language, requires a new type of catechist, one who is more a prophet than a classical scholar.[18]

Audio-visual language can best be used by those who have eyes to see and ears to hear. This does not mean those who see superficially or hear every sound wave that is produced, but those who can see what the eye has not seen, and hear what the ear has not heard. The Bible says of Moses: "It was as if he saw the invisible." (See Heb. 11:17)

Audio-visual catechesis does not consist in illustrating a talk or in presenting things materially with Kodachrome. It aims at expressing the meaning, the possibilities, and the deep human issues in man's life. In order to achieve this, catechists need more than information and doctrine. They need a faith that enables them to go beyond the obvious and to recognize the ongoing revelation of God.

A consideration of photography and music will enable us to understand more clearly this need for catechists who are men and women of vision.

---

[18]In this context "prophets" are understood as men really living within the structures and forms of their times. This incarnation is the necessary condition for a genuine transformation of reality. Prophets are not men brandishing the Word of God from above, but those who make us see the depth of things and who bring out in today the beginnings of tomorrows.

Photography:

V. Jiru, editor of the Czechoslo-
vakian *Fotographie,* comments
on the work of Czech photographer Jiri Macak:

*Macak . . . confirms my view
that the creative photographer
must cultivate his eye for the
essential in his surroundings, in
his fellow human beings, and in
life in general: if he hopes for
recognition, he must be both a
seeker and a finder. A photographer who discovers and expresses an unusual charm and a
new magic in a simple everyday
subject earns our sincere grati-
tude.*

*There are only a few artistically
active photographers who recognize that all art—and not only
photography—depends on a rejection of realism, on a poetic recreation and not the mere reproduction of what the artist sees
or experiences. Jiri Macak understands this truth and acts accordingly—whether consciously
or subconsciously is not import-
tant. He is an artist for whom
objective reality gives the im-
pulse to the creative act, to visual
creation. I can well imagine that
Macak chose a subject as simple
as the egg mainly because he
found in it the welcome opportunity of trying out his capabilities and of testing to the utmost
the individuality, sensitivity and
emotional strength of his artistic
powers.[19]*

A similar description is given of
the audio-visual writing style of
J. M. le Clezio:

*He is a visionary of a very rare
acumen: reality seems to besiege
him from all sides at once. He
depicts it with a very precise
realism; then suddenly he seems
to see through appearances of
things and people and to go beyond the obvious to what is
unique.[20]*

---

[19]*Camera* (Ed. Boucher, S. A.
Lucerne, January, 1969), n. 1. p. 14.

[20]*Realities* (Paris, March, 1969),
pp. 103-105.

52

Music:

Karlheinz Stockhausen describes the composition of his great orchestration "Carre":

The first rough drafts were made aboard planes during a six-week tour of the United States towards the end of 1958. Traveling above the clouds, I became intensely aware of the slow pace of material change and of the immensity of space.[21]

From this point on, Stockhausen "saw beyond," became completely involved, and amplified reality by attuning it with the depths of human consciousness. His orchestration then expresses the possible meanings, new horizons, powerful emotions, and ever-present hopes which surfaced for him when flying above the clouds. Stockhausen's orchestration is in a certain sense a prophetic interpretation of reality. It is this kind of vision, capable of proposing a spiritual or religious significance to all life, which is essential to catechetical audio-visuals.

Some people feel that their greatest difficulty in using audiovisuals in catechetics is the technical knowledge required to use the instruments effectively. Actually, most people can easily overcome this difficulty with a little practice. Far more exacting is the creating of a script, the combining of sounds, pictures, and words which will be spiritually significant. Herein lies the real challenge, and such a task requires prophets rather than technicians, artists rather than logicians.

Is audio-visual language capable of expressing faith?

The real problem lies not with limitations of audio-visual language but with the limitations of our faith. In order to use audio-visual language effectively in catechetics, we need

1) men of vision
2) a new type of Christian life and community, resembling closely the early Christian communities.

---

[21]Excerpt from Deutsche Grammaphon's "Avant-Garde," collection in the *Music for Today* series.

chapter 4

audio-visuals and revelation[1]

H. KUNZLER

[1]While there is a similarity of
inspiration and approach between
the preceding chapter by Pierre
Babin and this chapter by H.
Kunzler, a pastor of the Reformed
Church, there are differences
which can be mutually enriching.
Each author has his unique personality and religious tradition; consequently, there will be varying
emphases, nuances, and stresses.

Although "catechisms" have traditionally been judged by their doctrinal orthodoxy, the pedagogical dimension is rightly being given an increasing importance. Since any critical evaluation of religious education has a double point of reference—faithfulness to the Word of God, and faithfulness to the one receiving it—we cannot first of all present a doctrinal expose of the faith and then seek pedagogical means for its proper assimilation. To do so would make us unfaithful to Christ the Mediator, since the message and the medium are inseparable elements of the one proclamation.

At first sight, evaluating audio-visuals for religious education would seem to be merely a technical problem. But there are doctrinal implications as well: Is our pedagogy that of Christ? Can the *Mediator* we want to serve make His the media we use? Will they betray Him? Can His message be incarnated in them and present us a better understanding of Him than in the past?

Religious educators must be aware of the impact audio-visual media have on modern man.

Only recently have we come to realize what impact the media are having on our world, and how extensively these technical extensions to our sensorium are affecting our ways of knowing and acting. Because they have invaded and transformed our world, printing, electronics, and photography have also become mediators in the learning process. Although the media transmit knowledge, they do so with a bias; they translate, but in so doing betray; they reflect, but also diffuse like a prism. They are the prerequisite and the condition of our knowledge, yet they are simultaneously the cause of its distortions. Any communication of the Word of God through audio-visual means therefore will obviously both gain from the assets, and suffer from the liabilities of the use of such media. Consequently also, whether the catechist chooses to use them or not, the media and technology currently permeating our world must come under close theological scrutiny.

In a civilization of print technology, there is a danger of making faith an ideology, a system of thought, a question-and-answer type of synthesis.

Religious education and ideology

Religious education, because of its dependency on a visual culture where the printed word has been almost the only medium of communication, runs the risk of essentially distorting Revelation.[2]

---

[2]This is well brought out in Hendrik Kraemer's analysis of preaching in the light of changing communications environments:
"The extravagant and nearly exclusive stress on verbal communication, on preaching and sermonizing, in the world of the Churches, which issued from the Reformation, is a degeneration or distortion of the Reformer's discovery of the prophetic character and quality of the Word of God. This stress has closed the eyes of the Church to the manifold means of communication which we find in the Bible, which in contradiction to our

Western World is not confined to,
or imprisoned in a "verbal
Culture." The leading idea in
elaborating the many Biblical data
or allusions to possible means of
communication would have to be
that of the Bible's natural tendency
to take fully seriously the fact of
man's wholeness and diversity.
One of the important conclusions
of such an elaboration would be
that the current conception of
communication—that is, how to
communicate the Gospel in a
language that the secular man can
understand—as one of the great
contemporary problems of the
Church is too narrow and one-
sided. Of course, this aspect is
implied in the problem, but it
is only one aspect and probably
not the most important for the
reason that the Christian message,
which must be communicated has
such deep and wide dimensions
that they transcend the territory
of verbal culture, howsoever re-
fined and high its standard may
be. And for another reason also,
namely that the critical and ques-
tionable *(fragwurdig)* situation of
the Christian Church and message
in the world of today must be met
by many more and different
means than that of more compre-
hensible language."
Hendrik Kraemer, *The Communication of the Christian Faith*
(Philadelphia: Westminster Press,
1956), pp. 27-28.

Everyone is aware of the grave crisis presently faced in preaching and in other areas of religious education. The catechism has too often been a series of answers to questions which no-one seriously asks any more. As such, it has been the elaboration of what has been called a Christian catechetico-ideological system. What has been disastrous is that all too often adherence to this system has been, and to a certain extent still is, identified with faith-understanding. Of course, other areas of human understanding have also become ideologies or systems of thought that impose themselves upon us. But this merely underscores the need for a theological and critical evaluation of media within such a context.

Placing sight in a privileged position among the senses makes us relate to our world in an unreal way.

McLuhan affirms that phonetic literacy has given sight an unusual predominance over the other senses and, as such, has basically restructured our grasp of reality. Through print technology, words have become objects of vision. Man slowly but surely became immersed in a visual, book culture. There is quite a gap between Gutenberg and Marconi. But during this time man gradually forgot how to hear and feel his world, he learned to retranslate all of its realities into visual terms.

Characteristic of the visual approach to understanding is its emphasis upon continuity, quantity, and logic. The notion of three-dimensional space, for example, is conceivable only within such a system. However, the world our other senses encounter is discontinuous, qualitative, and paradoxical.

Really knowing our world also means hearing it, touching it, feeling it.

When sight unduly predominates and thereby causes the other senses to become atrophied, it is possible for us to create a unified, 3-D vision of our world. On the contrary, when our senses are more equally active, the multiplicity of impressions received are joined together in a more realistically patterned mosaic. The unity achieved is the result of the active interplay of our sensory perceptions. Without this interaction, knowledge based merely on the visual tends to become overspecialized. While such knowledge results in outstanding scientific or technical achievements, it also simultaneously produces a partial and distorted view of reality.

Historical consequence: faith-expressions based solely upon a visual type of knowledge.

Living as it has within a context of visual literacy, the Church, over the past few centuries, has quite necessarily couched its theological and catechetical language in visual and linear terms. For better and for worse, our knowledge of God and of Christ's message, as well as our teaching, have been expressed in a coherent, continuous, and stable language, in a one-sided system of thought devised to make it accessible to all. This has permitted us to give deserved stress to God's abiding faithfulness and to the universality of His revealed plan for mankind. But this has also caused us to construct self-sufficient systems of thought which claimed universal value and absolute internal cohesion and unity. While such closed structures were being built, vast areas of the world's life were being lived outside of them. As a result, the Word of God could not permeate and vivify them.

There is idolatry when we claim that one medium can give a privileged and adequate representation of God.

Realism or idolatry?

A valid though indirect indication for the theological evaluation of media is to be found in the scriptural injunction against fabricating idols for worship.[3] We can wonder at the seemingly absolute nature of this commandment. On second thought, however, the prohibition seems to stress yet another aspect: **no one medium alone can adequately express God.** Even with the best of intentions, the artist—in this case the sculptor—is betrayed both by his art and by the result obtained. In this sense, a clear and intellectualized concept of God would be as much a violation of the second commandment[4] as it is of the first. A God that can

---

[3]Ex. 20:3-6.

[4]Ex. 20:7, RSV: "You shall not take the name of the Lord your God in vain."

thus be comprehended and grasped, a God that need not be sought within our sense-world really deserves the sarcasm of the prophets, for he is an unreal and impotent God. Our understanding of God is precise, but false. And consequently our expression of Him is misleading.

The catechetico-ideological system we were referring to is obviously such an idol.[5] It claims to have a privileged view of reality, affirms its internal infallibility as a system, and rules out as invalid any outside questioning of its logic and values.

Opportunities for the Word of God could be missed if we remain enclosed within a book-culture approach.

Today, however, another of our senses, namely hearing, has been given an extraordinary technological extension. The electric media, by extending our capacity to hear as well as to see, have shortened the gap produced by print technology and relativized its monopoly. The weakness of a presentation of God which is based solely on the medium offered by a visual culture becomes increasingly evident. To continue presenting religious education in such an ideological context constitutes a violation of man and a

---

[5]Emil Brunner refutes such idolatry in these terms: ". . . because He Himself is the Word, and therefore can never be fully expressed in human words, no doctrinal formulation, however excellent, can claim to be the Word of God itself, or even the infallibly 'correct' doctrine, which has been formulated and laid down once for all."
Emil Brunner, *Revelation and Reason* (Philadelphia: Westminster Press, 1946), p. 153.

distortion of truth. Any objection of ours to such a catechetical approach is certainly akin to the scoffing of the prophets concerning the speechless idols of their times.

The God we know is more living and dynamic, and from Him we have received a call to make Him known to the young people of our world. We willingly catechize, but we are well aware of the inadequacy of such goodwill. Part of the inadequacy might just be in the medium we use, a medium fashioned by a book-culture, a language which expresses realities—even those of faith—almost exclusively in a visual, linear fashion.

The question is certainly much wider than the pedagogy and the media used within a religious education program. The problem is basically concerned with the changes required within our culture. Persisting exclusively in the traditional ways of communicating would only serve to perpetuate their shortcomings. Even if by some chance we were to succeed, we would only be perpetuating a partial and idolatrous view of God and of faith.

God uses a multisensory approach in revealing Himself to Man.

A multisensory approach

A second criterion for evaluating audio-visual media is given to us by the Scriptures: revelation appeals to all of man's senses.

The biblical message is not a continuous and homogeneous discourse. Here again we can speak of an impressive mosaic, where the mystery of God is uttered in a way that requires a variety of sensory perceptions. The tradition concerning Moses is more visual than the oral tradition of the patriarchs. Here the paths of oracle and vision meet and cross. Similarly, the homogeneous message presented by a localized and visible Temple confronts the discontinuity and magic of local forms of worship. But the prophets challenge this overprotective and impoverishing monopoly. For them, God is more and other than His Temple. Wisdom can only be found where the wealth of preliterate eras is integrated with the patient work of the scribes.

These same elements can be found in the New Testament. Christ is the Word and the Image of God. He alone perfectly reveals the Father, He alone is an expression of God which is not false or vain. In the temple of His universe, the Creator has made only one other expression of Himself, only one other "idol": Adam. In order to love his Creator, man will love his neighbor. He will come to know God through his fellowman. Such a view of man has of course prophetic and eschatological overtones. Christ is the new Adam, the one having attained perfect manhood, thereby restoring within us and in our knowledge of others the image of God.

In curing the sick, the infirm, and the lame, Christ restores them their physical and sensory unity. Thus, communication between man and man as image of God is made possible anew.

Christ comes to restore man's capacity for relationships. Indeed, man's whole being is involved in knowing others and creating relationships with them. And he relates especially by seeing, hearing, or touching. That is why, when Christ cures the sick, he restores to them the wealth of their sensory ability or their capacity to know and to relate as complete persons. The restoration of the physical and sensory integrity of the person is basic to each one of these cures. Having "ears to hear" (Mat. 11:15) is just as important as having "the ability to distinguish" (1 Cor. 12:10).

Even Thomas is not censured for wanting to touch. Thus, man's sensory capacities have a definite relationship to God's work and revelation. Furthermore, man is expected to fully integrate his senses in his worship of God and in his service to neighbor.

The technological extension of his senses and his increased mobility have given man a royal prerogative, a new level of dominion over creation. But noblesse oblige!—Man is responsible for what he does, for the use he makes of the tools, the machines, the techniques he has developed for himself. In fact, man has misused some of these by giving one sense a disproportionate predominance over the others. His technology now enables him to reestablish a healthier balance.

The revolution caused by the electric communications media offers us new opportunities for religious education, beyond those provided by print technology.

These media are used in our world, and consequently mentalities and ways of understanding are undergoing radical change. Adapting to this new situation will allow us to stress at least the following:

1 - **Knowing God means knowing man.** Reflection on the meaning of human experiences in the light of the Gospel leads us to God.[6] The use of audio-visuals as a catalyst for such reflection can give a decisive impact to religious education.

2 - **Knowing God** means seeking Him with our **whole being,** with the attentiveness of **all our senses.** Only in this way can the Gospel shed its light on the human situation and become revelatory for contemporary man.

3 - **Our knowledge of God has love as its only point of reference.** It is next to impossible for us to integrate the full range of our various sensory perceptions except in an eschatological context.[7] This, of course, necessarily confronts us with a world in which, luckily, hypocrisy is difficult: young people are very demanding when it comes to honesty. In such a context, the only

---

[6]This is the very approach used by Christ, as J. Jeremias reminds us. See his *The Parables of Jesus* (New York: Scribner's, 1963), pp. 115-229.

[7]See 1 Cor. 13:8-12. Knowledge and love of God are imperfect within man's temporal context. This context is one of growth, tending toward ultimate fulfillment in Christ at the end of time. Growing in this awareness and love occurs, however, in a temporal situation (see Mat. 25).

unifying factor for our knowledge is an authentic, though difficult, **agape.** Young people will believe us only if they are convinced that we genuinely love them.

These three points are obviously the very opposite of what is characteristic of a visual and linear knowledge of God (gnosis, catechetico-ideological system).

Two pitfalls to avoid.

Risks inherent in the use of audio-visuals for religious education.

It is important that we be aware of the risks involved in an audio-visual catechetical presentation.

A new despotism is possible: the predominance of sound could replace the tyranny of the visual: a sense culture could replace a meaning culture.

The first and most obvious risk lurking in the use of audio-visual material is that a developing aural mentality will simply replace the tyranny of the visual. Everything would be perceived in the manner of sound, and the sense of sight itself would become atrophied. We would become effectively enslaved by the dictatorship of sound, as is the case in nonliterate societies. We would be thrust into a world of discontinuity, a world dominated by sound and noise, a world where there are only "instant" gods, where the law of honesty forbids any kind of mental reservation, where truths substitute for the Truth, and where the magic of happenings replaces the worshipful quest of the One.

Nevertheless, no wistful longing for the values of a past and merely visual culture is going to stop this shift from a linear to an aural culture. It is a matter of equilibrium: we have to keep things on an even keel. Our task, now and in the future, is to keep a healthy tension and balance between the values of both cultures.

Sensory overstimulation can also paralyze our efforts in religious education.

Various media and techniques have a different impact on us. The resulting imbalance is something we must be aware of, since it constitutes a serious pitfall. Is it not possible that our capacity for active involvement has been far outstripped by the technological extensions we have given to our senses and the consequent flood of information this has produced? Are we so saturated with information that we do not know what to do with it, that we can no longer react? The use of audio-visuals in religious education could lead to such a dead-end. The use of multimedia could merely swamp us with information, creating a "spectator sport" type of religious education that would inevitably and effectively result in passivity and apathy.

This is a far cry from the goals of religious education, namely, the formation of community groups in which a growing collective consciousness will stimulate the development of decisive and efficacious involvements that go beyond the limited capacities of individuals and even of the group itself.

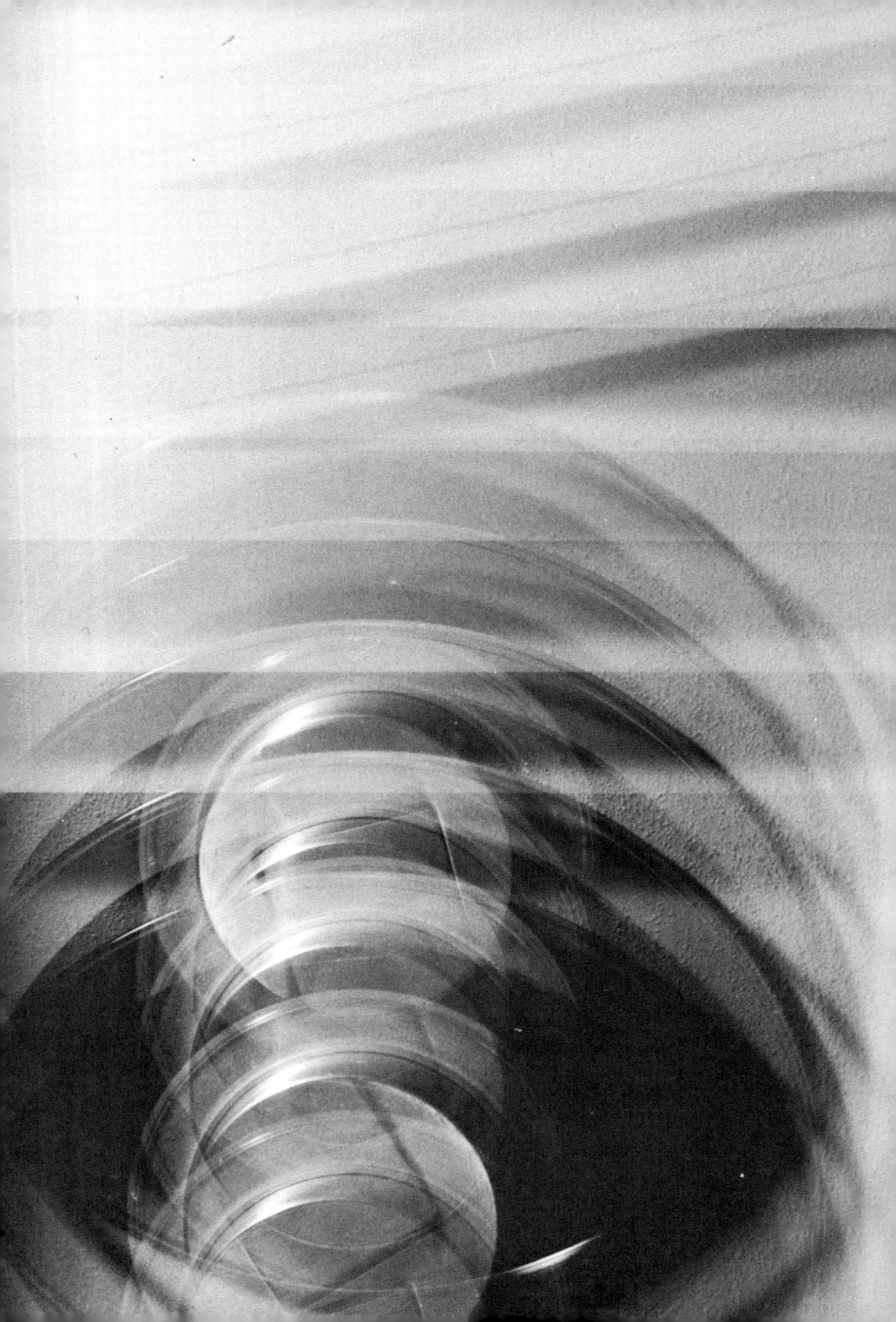

part two

learning a
new language

INTRODUCTION

Audio-visual language is a language of coexpression. What do we have to know about this language before it can become an effective means of educating adolescents in the faith? What are the basic elements of the language? How can we learn to speak it? Part II deals with these matters, and rightly so.

In fact, as catechists, we might ask ourselves why we should be concerned with reading and analyzing images and sounds, why such artistic or technical matters should interest us. The reason is that we cannot speak until we have learned the language. And to learn the language, we must first understand the importance of the play of light in a photo, the depth of feeling a sound can convey, and the poetic power of words.

Our ultimate goal is always to speak His Word to young people in their language. The coexpression of sound, images, and words are but the language in which His Word can be heard and understood in modern life. In His Word, image, sound, and words have a new and fuller dimension and meaning. Indeed, the Lord has explicitly told us that His Word will not pass away[1]. And again, He states: "The words that I have spoken to you are spirit and life."[2]

What is meant by the term "audio-visual"?

The term "audio-visual" has three different meanings dependent upon the context in which it is used —

MEDIA . . .

CULTURE . . .

McLUHAN . . .

1. "Audio-visual" MEDIA

We often speak of audio-visual aids, materials, or techniques. In this context, the words refer to the instruments of communication and the techniques they employ. They are called "audio-visuals" because they appeal to the eye or the ear.

---

[1]See Matthew 24:35:

[2]John 6:63, RSV.

2. "Audio-visual" CULTURE

The terms are also used to distinguish today's culture from the print or literary culture of the past. In this audio-visual culture, image, sound, and print are interrelated. Communication results from the interplay of all these elements, and not merely from one or other taken in isolation. This form of coexpression is multisensory.

3. "Audio-visual" McLUHAN

As a result of the writings of Marshall McLuhan, the terms "audio" and "visual" have acquired even more precise meanings in contemporary usage. The *visual* here is concerned mainly with the printed word, and characterizes a culture in which sight predominates. In such a literary or book culture, the sense of sight is isolated from the other senses and becomes the almost exclusive means of perception. This overemphasis on the visual forms man's learning patterns along analytical and logical lines and results in a detached and uninvolved approach to the world around him. In this same context, the word *audio* refers to a culture in which hearing is the main source of sensory perception. Sound is primary in such a context. Consider, for example, the world of sound in which non-literate Africans or other primitive societies live.[3] The primacy of sound involves and tribalizes them: they are immersed in a world of sound. For them, it is not so much a question of logical analysis but of in-depth personal experience.

In today's world, both **audio** and **visual** elements are being better balanced. The gap between the one and the other is gradually being dissipated. Both sound and sight are becoming integral parts of the learning experience of the audio-visual man.

---

[3]The same could be said of American Indians of not so long ago. Among the Dakotas, for example, when a newborn baby cried, the mother would repeatedly stop this by holding her hand over nose and mouth. From the very beginning the child thus learned that in hunting or in war his survival and that of the tribe depended upon sound and hearing more than upon sight or speech. The net result was the acquisition of a sense-perception which for us borders on the "extra-sensory." See Mari Sandos, *These Were the Sioux* (New York: Hastings House, 1961), pp. 23-26.

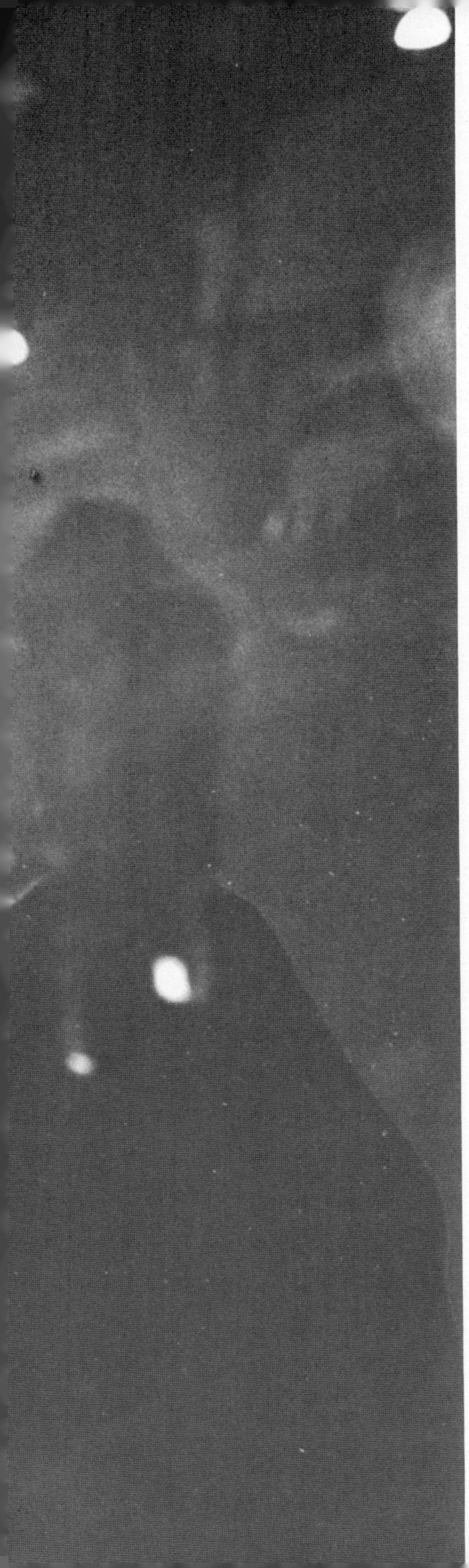

chapter 5

the audio
and the visual

MARC PETER

How do we learn to use our
senses in an integrated way?
How can we learn to associate
the **audio** and the **visual?** How
can we, as we enter a postliter-
ate culture, cease to give suprem-
acy to any one of the senses?
From the outset, it is important
that we concentrate on what is
specific to an audio-visual mentality, namely the integration and
interdependence of the senses.[1]
Consequently, we will try to distinguish what is characteristic of
an aural mentality from that
which pertains to a visual mentality. We will seek also to discover means to bring together
the elements of both a sound-
culture and a book-culture into a
unified audio-visual mentality.

[1] At least, this is what McLuhan
suggests. But can we really speak
of a total language, one involving
all the senses? There is room for
serious questioning of such a view,
especially concerning the senses
of touch and smell. Some recent
movie production experiments,
waggishly termed "smellies" by
critics, have been rather incon-
clusive. But the fact remains that
modern man has not yet said the
last word concerning multisensory expression.

In order to illustrate this integration of sound and word, we will begin our study with a consideration of an oft-used educational technique: the discussion of popular song recordings. We do so because, in song, the interdependence of these two elements of our audio-visual culture is evident.

Why do some song-discussion groups fail?

Young people usually enjoy discussing popular songs. These discussions center around the choice of records dealing with a common theme or artist. But the success of such "study" groups is far from assured; some are painful failures.

The reason for such failures or only partial successes is frequently due to the lack of active participation by all members. Once the discussion begins, many in the group fail to participate. Some even appear to be visibly bored. The group then falls apart—some continue to take part in the discussion, while others appear disinterested. A moment ago, everyone was involved in listening to a record; now, while some discuss the song, others prefer not to participate. A moment ago, there was a group; now there is none. What causes this? In most instances, the techniques used by the group leader are the most important factor determining the success or failure of the discussion.

The conventional approach is an intellectual one: "Do you like this song? Do you agree with the writer of the lyrics? What do you think of the theme developed? Would you have presented it otherwise?" A closer scrutiny of these and similar questions shows that the group leader has focused all attention on the words and the theme of the song. He would probably have proceeded in the same way if the topic of discussion had been a novel, a poem, or a Bible passage.

And the result? At times all will go smoothly because the group is familiar with this intellectual approach and at ease with it. At other times, the group breaks up as soon as such questions are asked because some are simply not interested. They have been asked to relate on a level with which they fail to identify: they were tuned in on a different wavelength when listening to the song. They listened just as attentively as the others, but now they either remain silent or evasive in their answers: "I like it, but don't ask me why." Or: "I like to listen, but I don't feel like talking about it afterwards." At this point the group has disintegrated. Some will follow the leader's questions and enter the discussion. Others participate only half-heartedly or not at all in the group exchange. Finally, such a division can lead to a marked hostility in attitude and even words. Those who have not participated consider the discussion useless. Those who have gotten involved are likely to consider the rest of the group dense and uncooperative.[2]

Effective discussion technique

The educator is largely responsible for the situation described above. The intellectual nature of his questions has, in fact, contributed to the splitting of the group. A product of a book-culture, he has remained within a visual mentality both when listening to the record and when starting the discussion.

By contrast, listening to a recording with an audio mentality means letting the song completely absorb you. Nothing else exists but the sound of the song. The hearer is totally caught up in the listening experience. In a sense, it can be said that he no longer exists—the song exists in him. Such an experience is the exact opposite of approaching the song with a purely literary mentality, in which the hearer retains a degree of noninvolvement, a distance between himself and the sounds he perceives. Here, on the contrary, the hearer becomes totally involved. His listening puts him into the world of the singer, that of the musicians. The climate of the song becomes his, a lived experience.

The educator who is aware of these characteristics of the audio mentality will then see the need for giving an important place to the hearing of a record. Also, the questions he asks as discussion-starters will express this same awareness. In preparing to discuss a record, the important thing is to listen, to listen again before speaking. The song must have time to permeate the listener, to become a part of him. Total involvement in a song is not automatic, but develops gradually. The hearer must be much less attentive to his thoughts than to his feelings.

---

[2]It is interesting to note a similar reaction to 16th-century humanism: "In the sixteenth century, the new book generation saw the oral and oracular, previous generation much as Polonius appeared to Hamlet. The razor precision of the oral schoolmen appeared to the new literary humanists as 'words, words, words'. They called the schoolmen not squares, but dunces." Marshall McLuhan, "New Media and the New Education," in *Christianity and Culture,* edited by J. Stanley Murphy (Baltimore: Helicon, 1960), p. 190.

But how then to introduce the discussion? First of all, it is imperative to avoid those questions which will lead to a purely intellectual response to the song. The leader's questions must focus on the group's emotional involvement with the record, not on the understanding of the song. They will go something like this: "How does the song make you feel? How does the record affect you, its rhythms, melody, tone, and/or voice? What kind of mood does the song create in you?"

Some will like the record, others will not. It is important that both groups have the opportunity to express their reactions. But it is not yet time to ask why. For the moment, the group is not engaged in logical and analytical reflection, but in the spontaneous voicing of impressions. Logic is incapable of expressing emotions and feelings.

A song is an unnerving experience: it happens to you and affects you at the level of sensation and emotion. What is "felt" is expressed much more easily by an association of many elements of perception than by a clear and distinct idea.

The evaluation criteria of a song might be summarized as follows:

A. In a literary mentality: all the questions focus on the "words" and the theme of the song.

B In an aural mentality: the questions are more diversified, but center mainly on the "feelings" of the hearer; they focus on rhythm, melody, and voice tone and quality.

Acquiring an audio-visual mentality

How is audio-visual mentality acquired? How do we go about integrating the aural and the visual? To study a song in such a context means asking those questions which the hearer can answer if he has *first* been permeated with the sound, *then* with the words. Such questions refer to an all-encompassing sensory perception where the audio and the visual elements have again become interdependent. The visual here is no longer isolated and therefore no longer confined by the limits of the analytical and linear approach of a book-culture.

The criteria for evaluating a song thus become:
1. Rhythm
2. Melody
3. Voice tone and quality
4. Lyrics or words

First place is given to feeling and emotion, then intellectual analysis. Involvement first, reflection later! You first let the song and its mood happen to you; critical evaluation will come later.

For most educators, christian or otherwise, such an approach to audio-visuals requires a fundamental change of attitude. For example, a discussion leader with intellectual-visual tendencies must come to accept and feel at ease in an aural mentality. Against his more natural dispositions, he must learn to listen in a global way, to live before analyzing, to "deintellectualize" himself.

As educators with an intellectual bent, we must squarely ask ourselves these questions: "Have we really accepted the technological revolution wrought by the electric media? Have we truly tried to adapt, or are we merely 'playing along', using audio-visuals but inwardly failing to accept them fully? Have we learned to get involved, to participate in ways other than the visual? In a song-discussion group, is our attitude more or less biased, that is, accepting of those young people who adopt a visual-literate stance while unsupportive or corrective of those who are immersed in an audio mentality? Is our goal one of understanding such people, or rather putting them on the right track?"

The audio-visual culture, then, stresses involvement, whereas the literary culture emphasizes detached intellectual reflection. A change in mentality is required, especially for the religious educator. The Church—if she is to promote involvement in and for the world—must speak to modern man in the audio-visual idiom which is becoming his most natural form of expression. Any continued neglect of the audio-visual culture will only accentuate the Church's inability to speak to modern man.

The importance of involvement

To have an aural mentality means to have a capacity for involved listening. Such listening leads to sharing and to identifying with what is heard. According to McLuhan, this type of understanding preceded the process of abstract analysis, which resulted from the invention of the phonetic alphabet and which was further reinforced by the invention of printing. Literary man learns in a detached way, while the audio-visual man is absorbed by and involved in what he learns.[3]

---

[3]The purpose of this study is neither to challenge nor to approve McLuhan's hypothesis. However, when he states that the invention of the phonetic alphabet is the source of man's disinvolvement from the world, the beginning of a decline in man's magical involvement with the cosmos, and the birth of an analytical and deductive secular intelligence, he leaves himself wide open to criticism. In fact, other hypotheses can be just as convincing, for example the studies of Von Rad, Bultmann, and Ricoeur on symbol and myth. However, we must also recognize that, more than anyone else, McLuhan has clearly distinguished the structures of involvement from those of analysis. Moreover, we recognize the value of his contribution in pointing out to us that the audio-visual media are beginning to retribalize and reinvolve man.

McLuhan illustrates the audio mentality with several examples taken from the life of the African Negro. Africans tend to agree with him. In particular, Leopold Senghor, President of Senegal, has described the black African as deeply sensitive and spontaneously responsive. This emotional involvement enables him to experience immediately the world around him.

Such an intuitive understanding is the very opposite of the white European's discursive reason, of his objective and conceptual analysis which places a screen between man and the outside world. The Negro proceeds by induction and intuition, others by analysis and deduction. Moreover, he has the gift of symbolism, of imagery and rhythm, and an extraordinary sense of communion and solidarity with the group.[4]

Characteristic of this is the showing of a film to nonliterate Africans: such an audience does not silently sit through a movie. The Negro likes to participate: in a scene where someone sings, the audience will spontaneously join in. The world of jazz and the worship of Negroes are just as revealing. A Negro does not listen to a melody with a beat in the same way as the average Caucasian does. Even when seated, he seems to be haunted by rhythm. We are all familiar with Negroes responding to the beat of a melody with their hands, their feet, their entire body. They do so spontaneously, rhythmically, but without any exhibitionism. For them, to become involved in a dance is as natural as verbal communication is for us[5]. Negro worship also shows similar signs of involvement: responses and interventions from the congregation are spontaneous and common. Even on records made by Negroes, it is easy to sense the interdependence of word, sound, and bodily rhythm.

The audio-visual mentality might be summarized in this way: the capacity to become involved through sound and visual image. It is characterized by an entire openness to the events of the outside world and an ability to let the tempo of these events enter into one's own life.

---

[4]From an article in the Paris newspaper *Le Monde,* January 31, 1968.

[5]"Africans will dance joyously at the slightest provocation: I have seen them break into an improvised conga step to the rhythm of a diesel engine with a faulty exhaust valve: one, two, three, BUMP!" John Scofield, "Freedom Speaks French in Ouagadougou," in *National Geographic,* vol. 130 (August, 1966), p. 198.

Audio-visual mentality and the Bible

From beginning to end, the Bible is concerned with involvement: through revelation and especially in Jesus Christ, God has involved Himself, He has entered into the history and language of men. Thus, if the Christian educator neglects the audio-visual language of modern man, he can rightly ask himself if he is being faithful to the Incarnation. The catechist must endeavour to acquire an audio-visual mentality. Such a conversion is by no means easy, since his theological and/or catechetical formation has, of necessity, been bookish. But it is nevertheless indispensable if the encounter with contemporary man is to remain possible.

As a result of the impact of audio-visual techniques on his life, modern man is more and more motivated by the need for participation and involvement. Any group of young people at a song-discussion session manifest this: Many of them quite naturally listen in an aural way. They are involved, they let the song absorb them. Like the African, at times their entire body catches the beat of the song. This increasing attitude of involvement has doubtlessly contributed to the decline of such classical dance forms as the waltz, tango, and fox-trot. Young Caucasians are not able to dance like Africans, and prob-

ably never will; but there is often here unconscious imitation. Despite appearances also, young people today do not dance in isolation from one another; there definitely is a collective involvement in rhythm and melody.[6]

Today, in discussing a record, the Christian educator is given an opportunity to change his mentality. Young people are in on the ground floor of an audio and involvement mentality. The educator must let himself be initiated into this "in-group" and let his "sacred" intellectual structures be challenged.

The place of concepts

Audio-visual techniques have re-introduced the audio mentality into Western culture. Must such a mentality, however, become the dominating factor? It would appear not. Let us return to our song-discussion to illustrate this point.

---

[6] It is interesting to note that the absence of such a collective involvement in Catholic or Protestant worship is a major factor explaining why young people are both uneasy and dissatisfied with religious ritualism. The same thing can be said of adult participation: it is extremely rare that signs of intense involvement can be seen on the faces or in the attitudes of a congregation.

There is a time for involvement, a time for analysis. Even if sound is primary, the words do not thereby lose their importance. The necessity of conversion to the audio-visual culture must not entail a neglect of the word. However, the word must be placed in its proper context: it does not come first, but last.

As has been stated above, it is important that an integration of the audio mentality and of the visual-literate mentality takes place, producing what we might term an audio-visual mentality. These should not be understood as two distinct and mutually exclusive approaches, but as two aspects of one and the same experience.

In discussing a song, elements of both mentalities will be interwoven. The group leader should first of all discuss the record at the level of feeling. The student is still completely absorbed by the mood of the song. There is nothing between him and the song; the song exists in him. In this first stage, this alone is important for the discussion. Gradually, however, the discussion should turn towards a recognition of the tension existing between the hearer and the song. The visual-literate mentality has its time and place: the flood of sensation and feeling must lead to a more reflective and intellectual understanding. Now is the time for questions on the theme of the song, its message and interpretation. At this point, the song may become a springboard for far-ranging discussions. The question is no longer "What do I feel?" but "What do I think?"

The importance of a timely visual-literate approach cannot be overemphasized. The Christian educator cannot stop short of it if his concern for adapting to young people is genuine. In this era of audio-visual techniques, some people stop on the way, and, remaining fixated in an audio mentality, fail to proceed to reflective analysis. Conversion to an audio-visual mentality does not necessarily entail the rejection of all the values of a visual-literate approach. If we speak of the wealth of global sensory involvement, this does not imply that we think analytical understanding is impoverishing.[7]

_____

[7]Although McLuhan insists that he tries to avoid value judgments, he is not altogether convincing. He gives the impression that, to a certain extent, he underestimates the analytical mentality.

Song-discussion groups are sensitive situations. Today, in most young people's groups, there is at least a latent tension between those who are determined to live in an audio mentality and those who have opted for a visual-literate attitude. The group leader must participate on that level with those who share this approach; it is part and parcel of the change of attitude required of him. During the second stage of the discussion, however, those who would tend to remain on an audio level must also accept to travel the road which leads to an analytical understanding: they too must accept to be open to visual-literate values.

The need for detachment

The importance of this mutual conversion cannot be over-stressed. And the needed balance is often difficult. It means for example that, when listening to a record, both the young people and the teacher really experience the song. Having together let the song absorb them and happen to them, they can now proceed together to reflect upon it. In this way, individual approaches are respected. Moreover, this allows for greater mutual enrichment since a fuller audio-visual understanding integrating both sound and concept, involvement and reflection is made possible.

As was stated earlier, the Bible is an invitation to involvement. But it speaks to us, with equal insistence, of detachment. The Word of God became flesh but,

paradoxically, there remains a state of tension between the Word and the world. The folly of God is a scandal for the wisdom of men (1 Corinthians 2). The believer is in the world while not being of the world (John 17). St. Paul explicitly invites the christian to discernment (Philippians 1:9-10). Discernment implies a certain detachment that enables a person to objectively evaluate reality. Jesus demands more than a superficial hearing; He requires a reflection and penetration that goes beyond the obvious: "He who has ears to hear, let him hear" (Mark 4:9). It is not sufficient for a group to be absorbed by a record; the participants must also reflect upon its deeper faith meaning as well.

Mutually supportive roles of involvement and analysis

Audio-visual techniques, in spite of the wealth they promise, also risk submerging the man of today and tomorrow in a flood of pictures and sounds. Audio-visual culture has its abuses. Involvement should not lead to the domination of man by the sounds and images he perceives at every moment. This is no future threat: it exists now. Because man tends to passively accept all that he hears and sees, he really risks becoming a mere aconscious and uncritical consumer.

It is imperative that an education be provided to prevent man from becoming a victim of the audio-visual culture. The Bible, inviting man as it does as much to incarnation as to detachment, as much to involvement as to critical discernment, places the Christian educator in a position to contribute actively to such an education. The first step is involvement: the realities of sound and picture naturally permeate man and seize him from within. The next stage is discernment: the individual sorts out and organizes what he has seen and felt and, thus changed in his innermost self by what he has perceived, is enabled to further communicate and act.

A second reason underscores the need for acquiring an integrated audio-visual mentality. Christian responsibility and involvement presuppose reflection and understanding. Can a person responsibly commit himself to something from which he does not have a certain amount of detachment?

Finally, it is important to note that this era of technology was born from man's capacity to step back, to be detached from his world. The conquest of the universe requires that it be considered as an object to be explored. Similarly, if audio-visual technology is to be valuable and continue to progess, it requires the maintenance of a mentality which is the very opposite of what it produces and in which it threatens to imprison man. Audio-visual techniques have reinserted man into structures of involvement. But, paradoxically, their development also depend upon detachment and analysis.

Coexistence of the audio and the visual—a modern necessity

The aural and visual-literate mentalities therefore must mutually interact and complete one another. Such an integration is what we have called the audio-visual mentality. The Bible itself exhorts to such a reconciliation: incarnation, critical discernment. Involvement makes possible situations, decisions, and commitments which are close to the world and thereby more fully relevant, while detachment enables more responsible action. To be in the world while not being of it: such is the biblical orientation given to man at the dawn of an era of audio-visual technology[8].

---

[8]The above contribution was written especially from a *consumer's* point of view. For a different perspective, see William Kuhns and Robert Stanley, "Coexpression and Religious Language," in *The Religious Situation: 1969,* edited by Donald R. Cutler (Boston: Beacon Press, 1969), pp. 869-895. Also, in this study another audio-visual medium could have been chosen as a focal point. The relationship of the audio and the visual in the film or television media would have led to much the same principles, but it would have been complicated by more difficult technical terms. The term *visual* would also have required considerable amplification and clarification. Confusion would have to be avoided between what is visual (what is seen) and what we have called the visual-literate mentality (the written word).

chapter 6

the use of sound in an audio-visual montage

ANDRÉ DUMONT
Producer, Studio RM
Cap-de-la-Madeleine, Quebec

The role and the place of sound

T.V.'s invasion of the communications field in the 1950's led many to believe that radio's death knell had been rung. Paradoxically, however, the transistor radio is an ever-present and typical fixture for the present generation. In the recording industry, too, business has never been so good. Concert halls and music festivals are playing to full houses. The sound revolution is on. Never before has sound been a more integral part of the human experience. It has more than ever found full citizenship in our present-day, turned-on generation.

We have just spoken of "experiences." It is important that young people "experience," "live," something together with the catechist. And we emphasize "live" because living, in all of its complexity, has a special value and impact for them. We can help them discover some of the meaning of life by a wise use of audiovisual aids. The aim of this chapter, then, will be to explore the possibilities of well-chosen and well-produced sound to increase the impact of a picture. This will be done by using specific examples.

A—The components of sound

1. SILENCE

Some situations really express the power of silence. For example, in observing someone talking, acting, making gestures behind a display window, you see everything, but you don't hear anything. The whole situation can acquire a new dimension that goes well beyond its usual and commonplace meaning. It can become poetic, humorous. You yourself recreate the scene, the events.

For many years now, the sound of song and of recorded interviews has been utilized in religious education programs for adolescents. Pictures, posters, and films play an important role. But each of these has been used in isolation. Now, however, the audio-visual medium is combining them. What then is the place of sound in this coexpressive medium?

It is of course important to note that sound need not accompany the showing of pictures or slides. What is important is that the presence of a picture or of a sound be justifiable. If a picture can produce the desired impact on the consciousness of those who see it, why add sound? Adding sound might only serve to distract and to disperse concentration. One thing must never be lost sight of: in our catecheses for young people, our aim must be to unify their experiences, not to distract them by our misuse of audio-visual aids.

Such an example illustrates the magical power of silence: it can be one of the best ways to underscore the meaning of gestures. Thus, in the production of an audio-visual montage, silence is not something to be avoided, but something to be utilized positively. Rather than being used negatively as a facile solution when nothing can be readily found to reinforce the impact of a picture, silence should play a positive, creative role. It will have value if it adds meaning and impact as a reflective pause after a stirring sequence in the montage. But it will be merely empty and awkward if it tells us only that the producer has nothing to say.

Use of silence in an audio-visual catechetical presentation: an example

In a multi-media presentation, a dramatic sequence shows Christ as risen, living now. **Abruptly, the sound track stops.** But the pictures continue: scenes from everyday life, pictures of pain and suffering, of scepticism and doubt. There is no need to explain. Everyone is struck by the weight of the silence which expresses the difficulty of belief. Such a silence is irritating, but effectively so in this case, since it compels us to reflection.

2. NOISES AND SOUND EFFECTS

The wailing of the wind always sends chills down our spine. A few seconds of this will immerse us more completely in a situation than could a whole series of pictures. Sound effects are shortcuts to the core of a happening; they identify us with the event. However, discrimination is required if the various kinds of natural and artificial sound effect recordings available to us are to be used effectively. Once the atmosphere has been created, we can reflect on the meaning of the event without needing an intense sound track.

One of the basic rules in producing audio-visuals is that situations should never be completely spelled out. It would be superfluous, for example, to reproduce all the details of an event. It is important to be selective, to insist on some sound effects, to play down others. Recent films have shown us that we need not be overly concerned with that kind of absolute realism which requires that each scene be minutely described by its accompanying sound effects. Sound effects should find their poetic climate-creating place in multi-media coexpression.

Example of a catechetical use of sound effects

A picture of Martin Luther King is projected on the screen while a narrator states that being a christian means getting involved, accepting to take risks for others. Suddenly, THREE SHOTS RING OUT. The entire dramatic scene of the assassination has just been recreated by the sound effects. They have violently thrust us back into the raw realism of the situation. A visual sequence could not so powerfully convey how demanding love of others and the effort to better their human condition in a christian way can be. A simple sound effect may have helped here to grasp a little better that Easter begins on Good Friday.

3. RHYTHM AND BEAT

Why does jazz captivate, move people? Many experts say it is because the rhythm is so close to our heartbeat, the basic rhythm of our life. A repeated musical beat has an obsessive, almost hypnotic quality that grows on you, leads you on. Adolescents particularly are immersed in such a physico-musical climate. When they dance, their entire body becomes an expression of fulfillment, joy, self-investment, or some similar emotion. A musical beat, even one without melody, can assure continuity between elements of a montage which we would ordinarily not even think of linking. Audio-visuals must speak to us, say things that are important and even things that we would not spontaneously wish to hear. Rhythm and beat may be most useful here. And sometimes all that is really needed is a set of drums, a bass fiddle, or a few guitars.

An audio-visual use of rhythm in catechesis

"The Church is not only me, but others. Christ lives in other people." As these words are being spoken, THE HAUNTING, REGULAR, ALMOST LITANIC RHYTHM OF AFRICAN DRUMS BEGINS, THEN RISES, while pictures are flashed on the screen. First, pictures from my land: a smiling girl, lovers, a family gathering, a beggar, a sick man. Then, an Ibo tribesman from Biafra, a wrinkled Eskimo with a toothless smile, a slum dweller from Bolivia, a church service in Germany and one in Vietnam, a ritual dance from the West Indies, a crowd protesting the injustice of racial discrimination, etc. The adolescent finds himself a quasi-captive because of the rhythm: he cannot help but see and somehow experience and accept what is being presented as encompassing the Church and stating who Christ is. The beat has taken hold of him, made him an actor in the drama unfolding before his eyes.

4. MELODY

Poetry remains one of the most important qualities of an audio-visual montage. Without that poetic quality of symbolism, ambiguity, paradox of multilevel meaning, a montage has little chance of speaking in depth to the adolescent, of bringing him to a stage of reflection. Without poetry, we merely spell out what he should think.

One of the best ways of introducing this poetic element in the montage is through the use of melody. The ideal would be to be able to associate the theme presented for reflection in the montage with a precise melody which can then be variously interpreted to suit the mood or situation.[1] It is not always a good idea however, to use a well-known tune since it may have too many connotations or previous experiences associated with it. It is certainly not necessary that the melodies used have the same professional quality as those played **in the Mauriat manner.** A new melody, composed especially for a montage by an adolescent and played simply and spontaneously on a guitar, is worth a hundred orchestral renditions of "Love Is Blue." Discovery, freshness, and originality are of the utmost importance.

Example of a catechetical use of melody in an A.V. montage

The group has just been listening to a song, in slow tempo, which underlines the presence of the risen Christ in today's world. After a brief pause, the music resumes, this time with piano and full orchestra, in a style similar to the sound track of the movie *Exodus*, while pictures of daily work, joyful happenings, etc., are projected on the screen. The impression is clearly one of growing victory.

5. SONG AND LYRICS

Any relevant program of religious education today must be close to the life of young people, their interests, and their way of expressing themselves. Youth-oriented radio programming continually brings out a flood of new songs, because songs have such a high impact rating on young people. Songs, in fact, bring out into the open a whole series of attitudes towards life which ordinarily cannot or are not otherwise expressed openly: the mystery of love, the beauty of nature .... For example, no sermon can bring out as poignantly and demandingly for adolescents the need to do something about the evils of the world as the song "Who will answer?"

---

[1] A fine example of such a use of melody is to be found in the film *Doctor Zhivago;* similarly, in *The Supper,* produced by KAIROS (Paul F. Keller & Associates, Inc.), 6412 Indian Hills Road, Minneapolis, Minnesota 55435.

As was the case for melody, young people like to hear at least one new or specially composed song in a film or montage. This is not always possible. But young people rightfully expect that certain songs should be identified with a definite theme or A.V. montage. Such a goal is surely worth striving for.

The use of song in an audio-visual context: an example

A series of questions on the problem of evil in the world gradually builds up to an intense peak, then suddenly stops. Instead of the expected cliche answer, a song suggesting another way of looking at evil, begins: "I was not there when you were in jail, when you were hungry . . . ." Such an approach will certainly have a great deal more impact with young people than the flat and prosaic answers we usually try to give to such a problem.

6. NARRATION

All types of narration can be used in an audio-visual montage. The two most useful types are: the documentary narrative, and what we call the poetic dialogue.

The documentary narrative presents a situation or explains the development of events in clear, concise terms. It is excellent for giving factual information and stimulating attention, provided it is not too detailed. This type of narration cannot be easily repeated. The facts have been presented, the situation explained: repetition would prove both useless and boring.

Poetic dialogue, on the other hand, adds a novel, interpersonal dimension to the mechanics of a montage. The sound track exteriorizes my conscience, how I feel, even the mixed emotions that co-exist uneasily within me. The ideal vehicle for this seems to be a dialogue between masculine and feminine voices. A poetic vision of life and reality is more important than the technical perfection of the narration sound track. We are convinced that poetry offers an unmatched way of seeing reality in depth. Many films mean very little to us precisely because they lack poetry. The secret of creating successful audio-visual montages lies in having and presenting a poetic view of life. This has the added advantage of respecting personal liberty because the attraction is based on aesthetic appeal and not on the impact of mere information.

Narration in a catechetical montage

At times the situation would require that a Gospel passage be read, and yet we realize that it would not have the desired effect. What could replace this is a contemporary-style radio news broadcast, with a commentator relating the events of the crucifixion and resurrection of Jesus. Or again, during the reading, two voices that keep nagging us with a verbalization of OUR most intimate feelings and questions: "What if it were true?" "How can I be sure that it is true?" . . .

7. INTERVIEWS

Through film documentaries and the daily T.V. fare offered to us, we have become accustomed to the interview as an effective means of rapidly getting to know personal viewpoints and convictions, expressed in an original and candid way. The interview then will be one of the best available ways to put life into an audio-visual montage, especially when ideas and personal viewpoints are involved.

In adolescent catechesis, it is important that interviews reflect the viewpoints of young people.

A montage will have impact upon them if they recognize themselves in the interview or have the impresion that their views are being faithfully recorded.

One great advantage in the use of interviews is that it fully respects the personal liberty of the hearer, his opinions and convictions. This will be so as long as the interview presents both sides of a question. We must be especially wary of using brain-washing techniques. We could easily be guilty of a biased presentation if the interview presents only an accumulation of one-sided opinions.

Of course, at times, the interview will be used briefly only to add zest to a viewpoint presented in the script. In such a case, the hearers will obviously understand that it is being used as a valid change-of-pace in the script and that in such a case all aspects of a question cannot be presented.

Example of the use of interviews in a catechetical montage

To begin a montage on "The Christian and revolution," why not make an in-depth survey, among young people, from a Christian point of view, on the meaning of race riots or student unrest on university campuses? This undoubtedly will be far more cogent than any well-presented thesis.

B—The use of sound in a montage

1. A FEW PRINCIPLES

Individual words are meaningless. It is how they are linked together that is important. Only a creative spirit can make them express, with varying tempo and color, a vision of things, a view of persons, an insight into the whirlpool of events. The same can be said in the field of the visual: rhythm and relationship control the way pictures speak to us. The use of sound is also bound by this law. We will have to take this into consideration when speaking of the use of sound in an audio-visual montage.

Creative imagination and variety are the only stable laws we can refer to in creating a montage. In this field, there is no other code of rules. It is more a question of taste, a question even of what is fashionable. In fact, to speak effectively to people living in a definite time and place, use must be made of those symbols, that style and manner of speaking which have not become dated from overuse. And that is in continual evolution. Contemporary films and T.V. commercials are still the best school for learning how to create a forceful montage.

As catechists of adolescents, we must also situate ourselves within their world. To what are they sensitive at the present time? How can we help them see certain realities in a way in which they would not normally do so? In a series of religious education periods, how can boredom be avoided? Here again, only one rule applies: variety.

The beginning of the sound track can emphasize one or the other of the components mentioned earlier. However, silence, narrative, and the interview should normally be avoided. The beginning of the sound track should be composed of those elements which are more easily assimilated and which create a spellbinding type of atmosphere: musical beat, melody, sound effects . . . .

Songs should ordinarily be the peak moments of the montage. Their impact is prepared and framed by the entire soundtrack.

If narration is used, care must be taken that it not become irritating. It must not constantly spell out what is being presented, but rather be discreet and poetic. The use of a dialogue form of narration will considerably alleviate the danger of becoming annoying.

2. SOUND TRACK BEGINNINGS FOR ADOLESCENT CATECHESIS: A FEW EXAMPLES

youth:
a) Discotheque music, loud

b) Voices: "Forget."
"Forget adults."
"Forget them: anyone over 30 is a square."

c) Music: louder, wilder

d) Voices: "Our parents don't make sense."
"Don't listen to them."
"Don't bother with them: come in at whatever time you feel like."

e) Silence

f) Voices: "But tonight you will be alone."
"If you're not there ..."
"I can't be young without you."

g) Whistle blast

h) Saxophone: a slow blues number begins softly

the problem of evil:
a) Voices. "We're a selfish lot."
"Sure, I'm selfish, but that's life."
"In this rat race, you have to look out for number one."

b) Song: "Skip-a-rope."

c) Newscast: City woman murdered as neighbors stand aloof in apathy. 3,000 Biafrans died today of starvation.

d) Sound effects: traffic noises or factory

e) One voice: "You can't hear people anymore."
"You haven't time to see others."
"Such is life."
"You really can't blame us."

f) Song (same as before)

g) One voice: "Whose fault is it? God's?"

the resurrection of Christ:
Dialogue interspersed with melody and song.[2]

---

[2]A useful guide and example would be the audio-visual montage, *Le gout de vivre* (A taste for living, produced by R. M. Studios (12, rue St-Denis, Cap-de-la-Madeleine, Quebec, Canada). Adolescent and adult views on christian living are contrasted, interspersed with songs and musical themes favoring reflection and interiorization.

94

sexuality:
Round-table discussion with a mixed group of adolescents, interlaced with comments from a similar group of adults and excerpts from current love songs.

living liturgy:
Dialogue, alternating with gregorian and folk-mass type music:

Voices: "A mass has to give you
    a sense of the
    beautiful."
    "A mass is not a
    concert."
    "Mass is not meant for
    individual prayer."
    "It's a meeting."
    "A celebration."
    "A sharing."

revolution:
a) Sound effects: sirens, fire
    trucks, and
    hoses

b) Shouts and screams

c) Slogans (distinctly heard):
    "Free students want a free
    university!"
    "Black power!"
    "Freedom for workers!"

d) Song: (on theme of human
    rights, discrimination)

e) Voices: "Is revolution
    christian?"
    "Yes."
    "Yes, it's christian."
    "Christ was a non-
    conformist."
    "Christ challenged the
    Pharisees."

f) Sirens, shouts (as before)

g) Dialogue (as before)

h) Song (as before)

i) Silence

j) One voice: "Are you all that
    sure?"

3. TECHNICAL ASPECTS OF THE USE OF SOUND IN A MONTAGE

As can readily be seen, the finished montage will have color, impact, and perspective inasmuch as valid elements will have been successfully integrated. And only those components will be worthwhile which produce these qualities in a montage.

Selection of sound elements for production

It is first of all important that the sound track for the montage be free from flaws and distortion. Good recording and mixing equipment is obviously a must. All components of the sound track should be recorded at high speed (at least 3¾ ips, preferably 7½ ips) to ensure undistorted reproduction.

High-speed recording will also facilitate editing and splicing. Unwanted noises, superfluous dialogue, etc., can be more easily cut out of the tape. This is important because any flaws or gaps in the sound track will definitely lessen its impact on the listener.

Looping of the tape, much as is done in film editing, will also greatly facilitate the splicing together and insertion of various sound elements called for in the script. The goal is continuity without superfluity.

Production and editing hints

The actual production of a sound track according to the requirements of the script may be done in a variety of ways.

One way is to prepare the sound track in continuity, by following the script and inserting the desired elements as they are called for. Besides requiring that all components be readily at hand, such a method presupposes that the technical producer of the sound track is very skilled. A major disadvantage of this method is that it often necessitates a number of retakes before the sound track will meet minimum requirements of quality.

A more realistic approach consists in prerecording all the required components of the sound track. These can be easily spliced together according to the instructions of the producer. If sound effects are to be added, this can be done with a sound mixer or adequate stereo-recording equipment. Dubbing and editing are greatly simplified in this way, and results are usually of higher quality.

We could add here a few practical suggestions. Insist on good sound quality for songs and interviews. Don't sacrifice the clarity of sung or spoken words to the desire to create impact or mood. Words must be distinctly understood. Otherwise, the hearer will become frustrated, since he cannot grasp rationally what is being said before being overwhelmed by the emotional impact of the montage.

C—audio-visuals: coexpression of the audio and the visual

Much has been written on the use of the visual media and on the creation of visual montage. Familiarity with the literature is essential if the audio and the visual media are to be effectively united for the catechesis of adolescents.

The components of sound in the production of a sound track have already been dealt with. A montage becomes complete when it becomes truly audio-visual, coexpressive, that is, when it speaks both the language of sound and the language of the visual.

96

1. IMPORTANCE OF THE VISUAL

To which does the producer accord more importance: the audio or the visual? Is it a matter of visualizing sounds or rather of animating a picture by sound? There are no hard and fast principles guiding this sort of precedence. Flexibility governs the choice. Consider the composition of a song. Within the same song, at one time melody becomes primary at another time the lyrics gain the ascendence. The composer's main concern is that the tune be catchy and the words expressive. The total effect leads to the following considerations: 1) generally speaking, it is easier to write suitable lyrics than to compose a worthwhile melody; 2) in the audio-visual montage of a song, people are ordinarily first moved by the music; and so, prime attention must be given to the melody in a montage, even if the lyrics actually came first; 3) words and music exert a mutual influence on each other, so much so that the music will at times require the rewording of a song, if the lyrics will cause a varying interpretation of the melody.

These same principles seem applicable as far as sound and image are concerned. The visual will ordinarily have priority: sound focuses attention on and enhances what the picture expresses. The viewer of a montage does not dissociate his sensation, but unifies them, ordinarily centering them on the picture or series of pictures he sees. Even if the sound track has more impact upon him than the pictures, it is not the sounds alone he will remember, but a precise picture linked with its accompanying sound effect. As a rule, then, the planning of a montage must center on the visual.[3] But this will not preclude the effective interplay of elements: in fact, the visual will influence the use of sound, and the sound track will to some extent determine the choice and the pacing of the pictures used.

Practically speaking, the production of a script for audio-visual montage will necessitate a variety of emphases. Care must be taken not to disperse our efforts or fragment the impact sought. Everything must be planned, and with a precise goal in mind. Sometimes the visual will take

---

[3]Exceptions, of course, are possible. For example, excellent results can be obtained by cutting the visual elements out of a montage at times in order to rely solely on the sound track for impact.

precedence; at other times sound will predominate. Whatever means are used, they must eventually center on the visual as the main point of attention: the picture, because it summarizes within itself the total impact of the montage, is what will be remembered.

2. IMPORTANCE OF THE AUDIO

Sound can literally transfigure a sequence of pictures. In fact, the same series of pictures could be commonplace and merely pleasant, or they may be disturbing, provocative, or restricting. A great deal will depend upon the sound track, its pacing, and the kind of enhancement or surroundings it creates for the pictures. The right use of sound is too often neglected. Unfortunately, producers yield too easily to the temptation of filling in the silent gaps in their script. Using sound effectively is a difficult skill to master, because of its largely unexplored complexities, and requires more time and patience than the choice of suitable pictures. The following example will illustrate how the same picture (or sequence of pictures) can be given at least four different meanings, depending upon the sound track.

3. VARIOUS USES OF SOUND IN A CATECHESIS FOR ADOLESCENTS.

The scene for the montage: soldiers in Vietnam evacuating wounded buddies from the battlefield.

Sound track 1:
war noises, moaning of casualties. This is the expected *cinema-verite* style, stressing the harshness already conveyed by the picture.

Sound track 2:
special newscast on the horrors of war. The information supplied has one purpose: to make or stress a point.

Sound track 3:
for example, Buffy Sainte-Marie sings "Seeds of Brotherhood."[4] This is an in-depth poetic reflection on the meaning of life, and the effort needed to make brotherhood among men a reality. How much remains to be done . . .!

Sound track 4:
cynical statements such as those made by a ranking U.S. Administration official: "We have to impress Hanoi with our staying power or they won't negotiate seriously,"[5] or by Vo Nguyen Giap, North Vietnam's Defense Minister: "The Russian Revolution cost 2,000,000 lives, so we can certainly sacrifice half a million people."[6]

---

[4]©1967 Gypsy Boy Music, Inc. All rights administered by T.M. Music, Inc.

[5]*Time,* September 5, 1969, p. 23.

[6]*Time,* September 12, 1969, p. 32.

What has happened in each case? In the first example, the sound track complemented what was being visualized. The second formula interpreted the picture. The third example established a dialogue with the visual. In the fourth case, there is a contrast between what is being shown and what is being said. In each, the same picture is used, but a variety of distinct audio possibilities produce four different effects.

Any quality audio-visual montage will take into consideration these laws governing the influence of sound on the visual. Painstaking efforts are required for worthwhile visual materials. Even though the results may be less immediately evident, the same kind of attention must be given to the quality of the sound track. Here lies the key to audio-visuals which will have impact on young people!

CONCLUSION

pictures that "speak"

How important, yet neglected, is the proper use of sound in audio-visuals for the catechesis of adolescents! Still, this is the key to any effective transmission of a life-experience. Finding good pictures for a montage is a time-consuming task. Why then expend even more energy in the extremely difficult task of creating a sound track to accompany them? Will young people really know the difference?

Indeed they will! Today's young people will be enthusiastic if the sound track has a "with-it" rhythm. But to generate this enthusiasm, you need pictures with shock value produced by timely sounds and silences, by well-chosen sound effects, by spellbinding musical rhythms, by expressive melodies, by appealing songs, by unusual narrations, and by striking interviews. The message of the Gospel can reach young people if we can enable them to become open to the Word. And that Word cannot find its total expression on the silent screen!

There is a whole new world to discover in audio-visuals, and we have scarcely begun to explore this area seriously. Audio-visuals can become a mode of expression, a tool for evangelization. Particularly when young people actively create their own montages, these can be not only a means to effective education but a means of faith-involvement as well. Pictures that "speak" for the "now" would be a step in the right generation!

APPENDIX

complementary aspects of picture, word, sound, and silence

PIERRE BABIN

WORD — PICTURE — SOUND

WORD—*A passing car.*

PICTURE—*"A car is passing."*

SOUND—*Sound of a passing car.*

Tautology and redundancy

No complementarity

Mere repetition

Basic elements in a montage
Like fire, water, and air
We have three distinct
  personalities
Each one of us has his own
  language
We don't say the same things
Or say them in the same way
It's a matter of harmony
Not of uniformity

According to time and place
One or the other will take
  precedence
But we do mutually influence
  each other
The ties that bind us are more
  like bonds of love
Respect our identity
Respect in us the fact that we
  complement each other

The West conceived the word
The East to the picture gave birth
Africa's child is sound

*The **WORD***
Herein the maximum of
  intelligibility
Of conceptual clarity, of cogency
Of formal exactness and of
  resoluteness

*The **PICTURE***
Emotion linked with thought
Atmosphere, yet quite intangible
The here and the beyond of
  things
An appeal to senses and heart
Ambiguity

*The **SOUND***
Arousal of an instinctive rhythm
Source of the physical experi-
  ence of fear
Of oppression, of turning on
Less mysterious and evanescent
  than the picture
It conditions the occult
It is the web or the clash of
  events
Or the direction that they take
It is the nerve-center
Of universal involvement

But what of the **SILENCE**?
A sister to all three
For the word, a cathedral
A time and place for prayer
A reflecting pool
A mirror for the picture
For the sound, a vault
An echo chamber
For each, an intimacy
Between them, a bond
With them, a recognition of
    uniqueness

**in a montage
silence is . . .**

Expectation

The silence of Advent

Midnight

Christmas—"While all things
were in quiet silence . . ."

Silence is a dark page written in
    white
Silence is a question
You can hear a pin drop
What does it mean?

In a montage
    SILENCE is
        a positive **SOUND**

Silence—A picture only—Eyes
Thought, reflection
I hear the pounding of my heart
And feel the rhythm of my
    breathing
Your meaning becomes my
    meaning
Your mind, your wishes
Your fears become mine

Silence of two lovers
Their embrace made public on
    the screen
Overwhelmed by silence
Silence where any sound of mine
    intrudes
I clear my throat
I become uneasy, fidgety

He has just told me the truth
    about myself
I stand naked
He has seen me
Silence of confrontation
Silence afterwards
On the battlefield
Night

Silence of friends
Walking side by side
The feeling is good
Silence after a meal shared
    together
Silence after communion
Silence of the earth
When the voyage is over

chapter 7

how to read
a picture

PIERRE PIGUET
BERNARD MOREL

A—The language of pictures

Pictures (photos, slides, drawings, paintings)[1] are objects with a meaning. They are **objects:** they can be handled, passed around, viewed or ignored; they exist independently of us and of our reaction to them. They have **meaning** because they are used to represent something, to transmit what a photographer or painter has seen and wants us to see. Their meaningfulness constitutes a kind of language.

There are many kinds of languages: some are visual and expressed by various signs or symbols; others are oral and require

[1] As indicated, this chapter deals generally with all kinds of pictures. For a more precise study of the language of photographs, see P. Babin, et al., *Photolanguage* (Ottawa: The Catholic Centre of Saint Paul Universiy, 1969, and Dayton, Ohio: Pflaum Publishing).

103

a hearer. Each of them is composed of various elements, defined by usage and convention, and organized according to its own grammatical rules. All of these elements are involved in the communication of a message. The language of pictures too, has its own elements, its own set of rules. To speak or understand this language, we have to be aware of its components and of their organization.

Today's written or spoken languages comprise a sequence of signs or symbols which form words, sentences, and series of related sentences. Their meaning is inscribed in a linear sequence having a beginning, a development, and an end, in a definitely patterned sequence. The structure of speech or written language is linear and temporal; the language of pictures, however, is atemporal. While a picture can suggest movement or even imply a time-sequence, these are not presented in linear succession; all elements become present simultaneously. Pictures, therefore, are not deciphered like speech. No grammar or syntax rules their structure.

Because their language is more suggestive than cogent, and their message more ambiguous, pictures must not only be looked at but interpreted as well. Such interpretation is immediate. Viewing the multiplicity of elements simultaneously has an impact which stimulates a personal and subjective response. We react without even trying to understand. We find the picture attractive or uninteresting, stimulating, or perhaps amusing. Visual perception is certainly not as objective as we may have been led to believe. Our very viewing of the picture is a projection of our own reaction; a good part of what we see in a picture is self-projection. If we see a picture as beautiful or interesting, it is because we are sensitive to those elements which convey beauty or interest. On the contrary, if the picture creates an impression of ugliness or boredom, we will tend to turn away and look elsewhere.

All personal reactions are unique. Taste, sensitivity, clarity of vision, training in perception, even level of education and cultural background influence our reactions. Two friends looking at the same stained-glass window cannot really grasp what the other sees in this work of art, since the response of each is modified by personal experiences. If we are not well aware of the subjectivism of our vision, we can be easily deluded. Were we mere "consumers"—perusers of picture magazines or photography collections—we could afford to be much less critical. But the responsible exercise of our role as catechists forbids us to use pictures simply because they appeal to us.

Since pictures constitute a language, our choices must be based on more objective criteria. Consequently, some objectivizing questions must be asked: What does the picture represent? What does it mean? What does it suggest? Of what value are these representations and meanings? A dialogue begins and grows— a dialogue which requires disciplined inquiry if subjectivity is to be controlled. The picture produces a subjective reaction in the viewer. He in turn tries to detect the objective content of what he sees.

The first reaction of a viewer has all the appearances of a **bias.** "First-sight" perceptions or impressions are a massive projection of subjectivity. They entail an unqualified judgement, sometimes expressed, sometimes not. The dialogue described above requires continuous referral to the picture if objectivity is to be maintained. The dialogue is concluded only when the viewer has satisfied himself that nothing remains to be discovered in the picture.

B—Can we be sure we have understood a picture?

A picture cannot become totally objective since vision is a subjective experience. However, when the objective elements are so discovered that the picture begins to speak to the viewer, it truly becomes a language. But it still remains an ambiguous language because the objective elements are understood in different ways by different people. There must be a constant dialogue between these two dimensions if the real meaning of the photo is to be understood. However, a complete absence of subjectivity is neither possible nor even desirable.

There is yet another reason why pictures remain ambiguous: they are an expression of what their creator wants us to see. Consequently, a subjective element— the result of a creative choice— enters into the picture and to some extent clouds its objectivity. What then is the meaning of what we see? Is it a reproduction of reality or does it convey a personal message? Both certainly, but with varying degrees of intensity, depending upon the type of picture. If the goal has been the production of an objective or realistic picture without taking personal motivation into account, then the picture will more obviously be a **reproduction,** and its interpretation will lie in that area. If, however, the artist wants to convey a personal feeling or an interpretation of reality, then the picture's **message** constitutes the major zone of importance or meaning.

The message transmitted by a picture is the result of a complex series of choices—most of which are reflex or unconscious —made by its creator. Choice of subject, of setting, of colors, of angles and perspectives, of lighting or of framing, for example, all contribute to expressing the artist's personal view of the reality he portrays. Reading the message of a picture will therefore require an effort to discover the intention of its producer. The only real clues we have of such intention lie in the picture itself.

Consequently, if we are not to be deceived by first impressions and purely subjective interpretation, a careful study of the choices made by the creator of a picture is necessary. In the field of photography especially, a good understanding of production techniques greatly facilitates the interpreting of a photo; the choice made at each stage of production should be closely observed.

Although a picture will always remain somewhat ambiguous, nevertheless genuine effort is important in order to discover its meaning. If we look too hastily at a picture, we will probably attach no meaning to it. On the other hand if we examine it too scrupulously, we run the risk of projecting upon it intentions it never had. In seeking the meaning of a picture, we must avoid both these extremes.

So far, we have spoken of the meaning of a picture. It might be useful here to establish a further distinction between the **significance** and the **meaning** of a picture. The significance or sign-value of a picture is to be sought in the picture itself. It lies in those choices that have governed the production of the picture and is very intimately linked with the actual physical structure of the picture. Meaning, however, is more of a subjective reality. It is discovered by the viewer who refers what is signified by the picture to his own subjectivity. Significance pertains chiefly to the visual document, while meaning is more a matter of decision on the part of the viewer. Obviously, meaning is far more ambiguous than significance, since it is more personal and less communicable, intimately tied up as it is with the viewer's subjectivity. Meaning is the ultimate word spoken by a picture, its inexpressible personal message, the unutterable insight which results from vision, the satisfaction of having seen.

C—Analyzing the structure of a picture

1. THE BASIC STRUCTURE

The **structure** of a picture is the ordering or the arrangement of the elements constituting the whole: colors, shadows and light, details of a face or landscape, and other visual effects produced by various techniques. The content of a picture is not only what the eye can see; it is also the result of preplanned and applied technique. Both these aspects must be emphasized. Actually, structure is to be found more in the **relationship** and ordering of the components of a picture than in the components themselves. It is the interplay of color, shadow and light in a setting of shapes and distances, as well as the relationship of details to their context and to the whole. The physical structure of the picture is constituted by this series of relationships.

This structure is not a haphazard affair. A picture reproduces something that is real or has at least reference to a visible reality. The structure of the picture reflects those artistic and technical means used by the producer. If these more or less deliberate choices are carriers of a message, then we can see the structure of a picture as a language, a means of communication between the producer and the viewer.

The physical, and therefore objective, structure of a picture is no one person's exclusive property; it can be used by anyone. In fact, we very often use pictures to communicate our thoughts: we buy pictures for use as greeting cards or for publicity purposes; we show pictures to friends in order to get their comments (instead of telling them about our holidays, we show a home movie); we use pictures educationally to illustrate a class presentation or to stimulate discussion in a group. The physical structure of a picture, observed and interpreted by each as best he can, is truly a means of communication.

2. THE ROLE OF WORDS AND CONTEXT

The ambiguity surrounding the meaning of a picture can often be partially removed by the use of accompanying words or commentary suggesting particular interpretations. In fact, pictures are rarely used without caption or commentary. The context in which a picture is presented is also of the utmost importance: the same picture will have different meanings according to the context in which it is seen. Some pictures have a built-in context —for example, the use of slogans and captions in magazine photography. In other instances, the

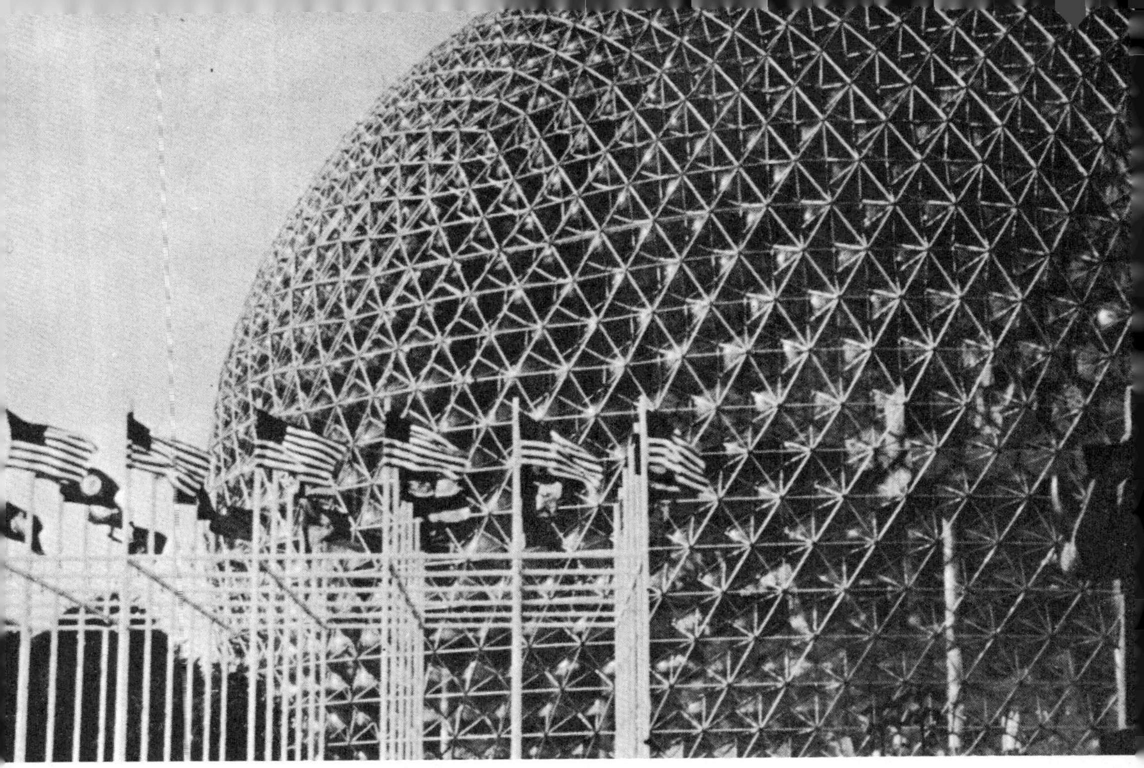

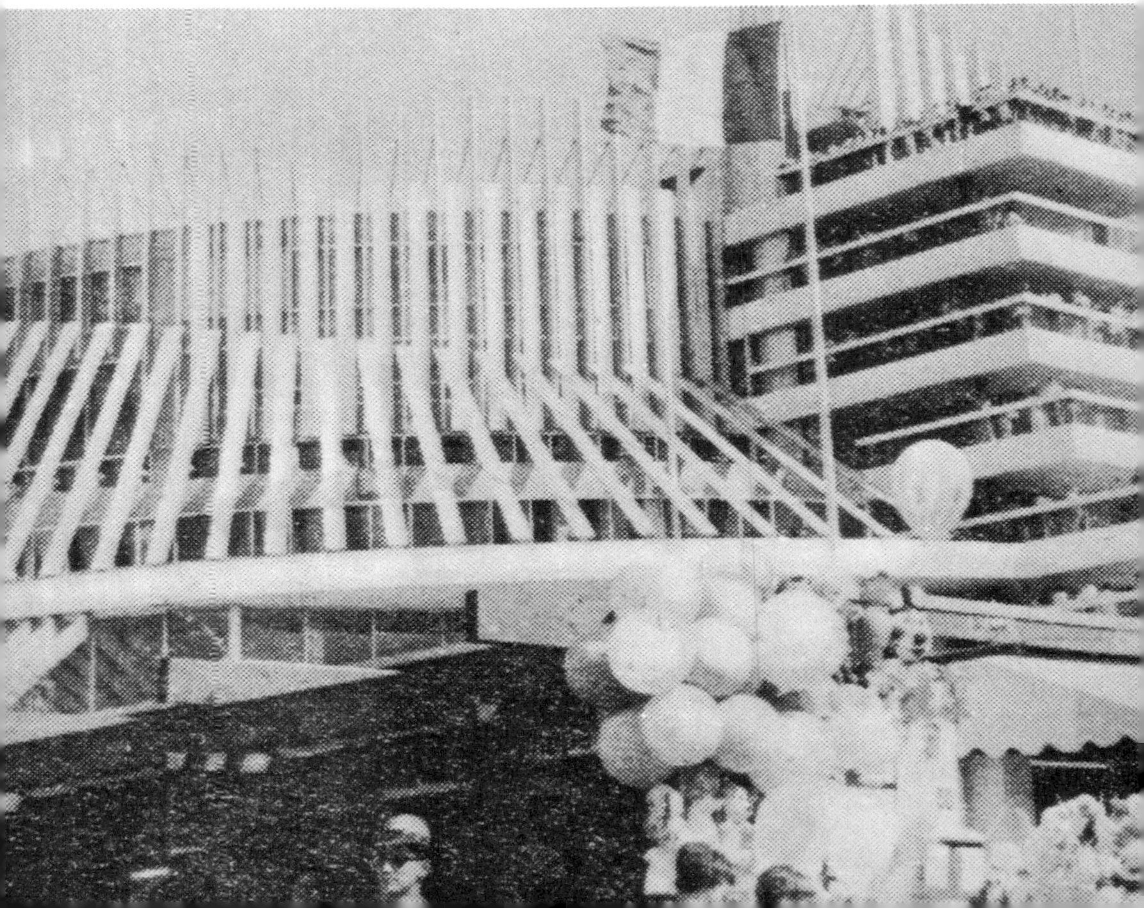

"Pure communication"

*"Freedom means living
in a prison
of one's choosing"*

producer has no control over the context: for example, the mood of the viewer or the lighting conditions under which the picture is seen. No picture is without some context of this kind. Whatever the context, it contributes to the interpretation of what is seen. Pictures produced without comment or caption are, of course, more ambiguous. What is seen is left to the widest possible range of subjective interpretations. The viewer chooses what he wants to notice, what he likes, what he understands; such choice is purely subjective.

Contrasted opposite are pavilions featured at Canada's Expo '67: those of the U.S. and France. The American pavilion was described as a "prison" while the French pavilion was labelled "pure communication." These, of course, were purely subjective interpretations. Actually, the American pavilion was in no sense a prison, especially not in the manner described by the caption above. On the other hand, many of those interviewed found the French pavilion, although beautiful, stark and rigid. Thus, another journalist with other biases, could very well describe the French pavilion "A porcupine," and the American "A world of light." This illustrates the importance of the words which accompany a picture.

3. SYMBOLISM OF THE PICTURE

Pictures, because they can be interpreted in such a variety of ways, are ambiguous. The more ambiguous they are, the more **symbolism** they carry. Symbolic pictures communicate, but in multilevel fashion. This is by no means a disadvantage. In fact, their very symbolic value is what gives them impact, for they are bearers of many potential meanings. Decision and choice cannot be made without hesitation. In such cases, a picture is richly laden with symbolism. On the other hand, if a picture contains little mystery or receives a good deal of clarity from its context, it is poor in symbolism. The more symbolism present in a picture, the more challenging the interpretation. Such pictures can be the springboard to endless discussions. What they lose in precision they gain in suggestive value, and acquire a greater capacity to stimulate the viewer's subjectivity.

Documentary illustrations—news items and scientific releases—generally lack symbolism. Works of art, however, are far more likely to be rich in symbolism. Pictures produced for scientific purposes strive mainly for accuracy: therein lies their documentary value. Occasionally, however, their beauty can be most thought-provoking.

IN SUMMARY

Structure

The **structure** of a picture is the result of the producer's selection of technical means to portray specific elements of reality. In final analysis, structure is "what has been chosen for us to see." It is the objective fulfillment of a personal plan or design.

Message

The complex interplay of these choices constitutes the **message** conveyed by the picture. Our essential task is to discover through the structural elements, the innermost motivations of its producer.

Language

The **language** and the structure of a picture are intimately linked. Not having precise grammatical rules, this language is vague and ambiguous. Its message is far from precise, and is only grasped in an approximate fashion.

Subjectivity

Subjectivity is a twofold reality. In creating a picture, a producer is incapable of expressing the totality of his subjective intentions. Similarly, the viewer projects his own subjective interpretations onto the picture when its meaning is not clear or precise enough. Since subjectivity remains a permanent source of misunderstanding, discipline is necessary in viewing pictures.

Symbolism

A picture speaks not only to the intelligence, but especially to one's sensitivity. Its purpose is to move emotionally as well as to illustrate, depending of course on the type of picture. Structural analysis of the picture could be carried too far. Its **symbolic value,** its basic mobility and ambiguity must be respected.

Choosing pictures for use in audio-visuals will therefore be a demanding task. Pictures cannot be used indiscriminately, without respect for circumstances and context. A picture will be chosen because it is suitable for whatever purpose we have in mind. To be sure it fulfills that purpose and avoids the insufficiency of selection on the basis of first impression, careful consideration must be given to analyzing the structure of the picture.

D—How to analyze the structure of a picture[2]

How can we read a photo? How can we decipher the message it conveys?
Two dimensions are of importance here:

a) the technical elements used by the photographer to take the picture;

b) the objective elements chosen by the photographer for his photo.

Analysis of the structure of a picture will necessarily involve a consideration of each of these dimensions and of their respective components.

1. The technical means chosen by the photographer

No picture is ever a mere reproduction of reality. Each of the steps in taking a picture becomes a mediation between the object photographed and the resulting reproduction. Each step is a re-interpretation of the basic datum. The photographer uses his art and the technical means at his disposal to direct this reinterpretation in the manner he chooses. Here are a few examples:

---

[2] The discussion will be limited to photography, since it is the central problem in modern audio-visuals. A similar study of painting and the other visual arts would however be useful.

111

a) Choice of lens

Let us examine photograph #22 of the *B* series of *Photolanguage*.[3] The photographer's intention is manifest. He wants to present a steam shovel in such a way that the gigantic proportions of its arm and claw stand out in order to magnify its power. To obtain this effect, use was made of a wide-angle or fish-eye lens, that is, a lens capable of encompassing in its scope a very large portion of the horizon. A wide-angle lens permits rather close proximity to the object photographed while capturing it in its entirety. Perspectives are therefore greatly accentuated, even distorted; distances and depths are exaggerated, foreground and background dimensions acquire marked contrast. Such distortion affects not only the steam shovel in the picture, but the buildings as well: their vertical lines tend to converge. The effect produced by wide-angle photography is widely used in advertising automobiles or restaurants for example. Much is to be gained by showing them larger than their actual size.

[3]See above, footnote 1.

On the contrary, a publicity shot for a city with mountains in the background will require a different approach. A telephoto lens will be used in order to create the impression of proximity to the mountains. Since only a narrow horizon is possible with a telephoto lens, the picture will have to be taken at some distance from the city also. The result will be a telescoping of distances and perspectives, and the nearness of the city to the mountains will be accentuated.

b) Picture angle

A photographer is always in some spatial relationship with his subject. The best angle from which to shoot the picture will be determined by what he wishes to emphasize.

Two examples will illustrate the main picture angles used: the high-angle shot (camera above subject) and the low-angle shot (camera below subject).

Consider, for example, photo #20 of *Photolanguage*, "B" series. This is a typical low-angle shot. The comments of young people to whom the picture was shown are quite meaningful: "Ruler of all. But what about God?" (Girl, 17); "The glory of man who betters himself through science." (Boy, 18).

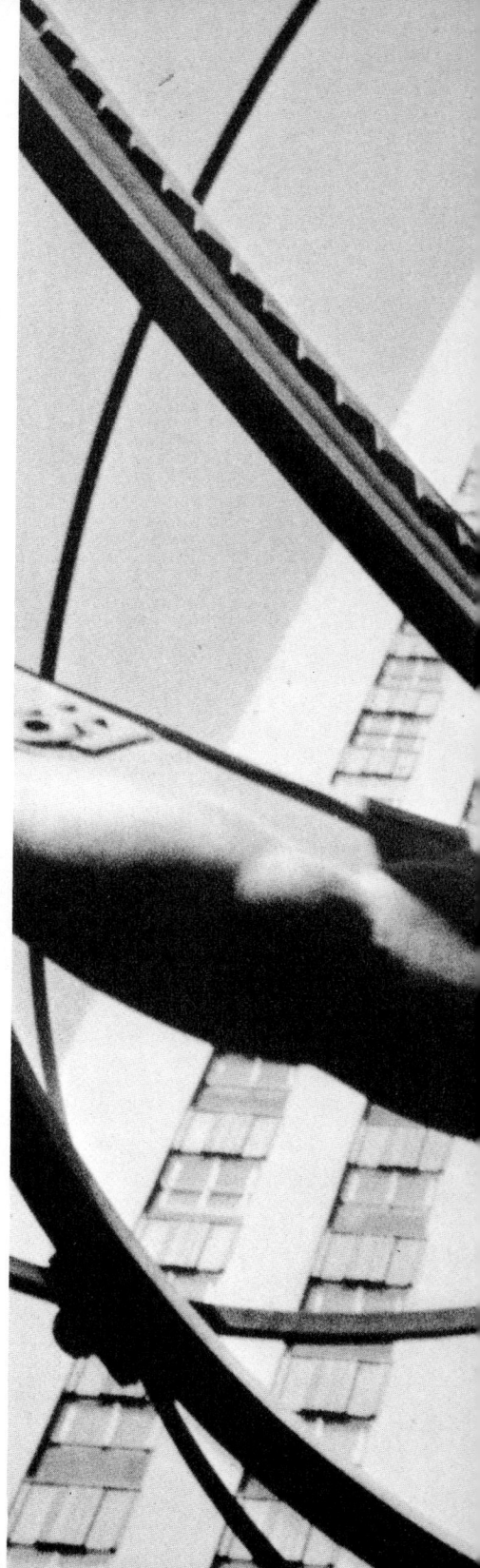

Now, suppose that the picture had been taken from one of the windows of the skyscraper in the background (high-angle shot). The impression of domination conveyed by the previous picture would partly, if not entirely, disappear. The sculpture would be crushed, and hardly discernible from the ground on which it stands. The picture we are looking at, however, makes us spectators admiring their own power in the works they have created. In the other case, we would become "God, measuring the distance that still divides man from Him." One thing is certain: the reactions and comments of viewers differ according to the angle of the shot.

The effect created by the previous picture can be toned down if the low-angle is less pronounced. Such is the case of photo #9 of *Photolanguage*, "A" series. The following comment to such a picture is quite typical: "She's looking down at me. Has she no one to look up to?" The photographer has most vividly captured an expression of arrogance by placing himself below his subject, thereby having her dominate us, "look down" upon us.

117

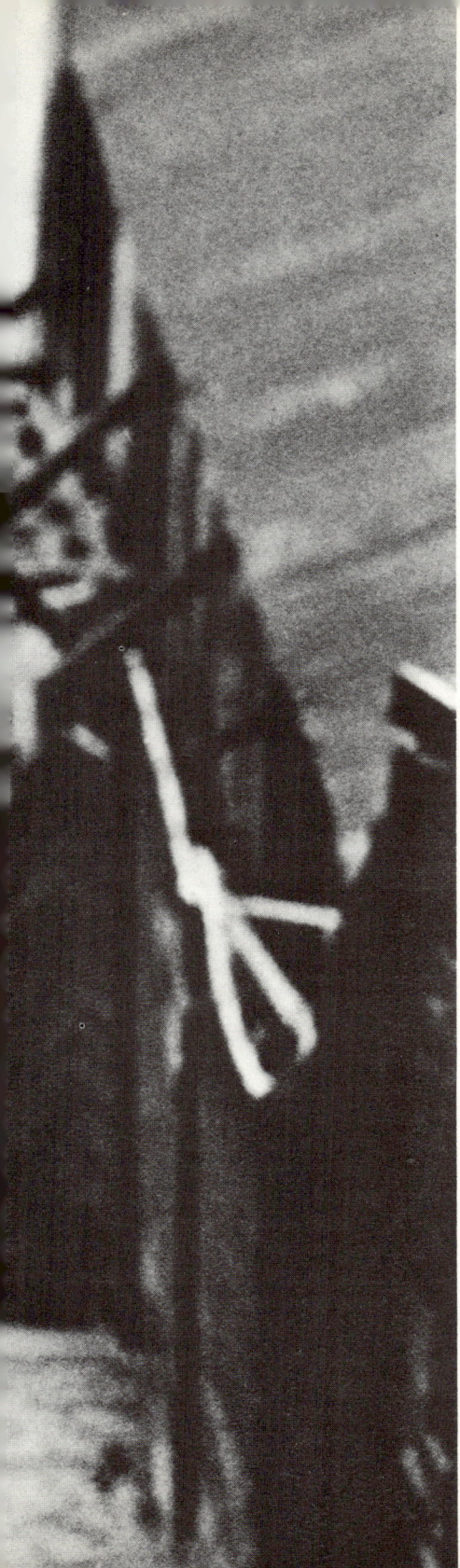

Photo #26 of *Photolanguage*, "B" series, on the contrary, is a high-angle shot. The appearance of the man is not too reassuring. We see him as fleeing, and seemingly crushed by his world. His state of wretchedness and destitution strikes us first; only later the suggestion that he might be dangerous occurs. If this were a low-angle shot, our fear of the man would grow and our feelings of compassion diminish.

c) Picture sharpness

The sharpness and clarity of a picture may vary. Lens settings here are of prime importance.

To obtain a sharp picture of a fairly flat, nonmoving subject, turn the camera's focusing ring until the distance shown corresponds to the distance between the camera and the subject being photographed. This assures the proper focusing by varying the distance between the lens and film. By this simple technique, the main subject will then be in sharp focus. But what of the other objects photographed, those in the foreground and background, especially if the picture has been taken at a short distance? These will tend to be blurred, because they are not within what is called the range of sharpness. The range of sharpness is that zone, in front of and beyond the main point of focus, where objects will stand out clearly. This zone or range is determined by two factors: the focal length of the lens[4] and the size of the aperture or diaphragm.[5]

A proper use of these technical factors allows a photographer to compose a picture as he likes. In picture #22 of the "B" series of *Photolanguage*, the range of sharpness, practically speaking, goes from the immediate foreground to infinity. By contrast, in *Symbolical Photo*[6] 505, the camera was intentionally focused on the boxer's fist, so that it alone falls within the range of sharpness, while the figure of the boxer remains blurred and enigmatic.

---

[4]The focal length of a camera is the distance from lens to film. This can vary considerably: for example, an extreme wide-angle lens could have a focal length of 17mm., while a telephoto lens could be as high as 200mm.

[5]The lens diaphragm, like the iris of the eye, regulates the amount of light admitted through the lens. Most cameras have their lens openings in terms of f-numbers. An f-number is determined by dividing the focal length by the diameter of the lens opening being used. For example, $f/11$ means that the focal length is 11 times the lens diameter.

[6]Available in Canada from Novalis, 1 Stewart Street, Ottawa 2, Ontario; in the U.S.A., from Geo. A. Pflaum, Publishers, Dayton, Ohio 45402.

Of similar interest is *Symbolical Photo* 531. Here, however, the background is sharply focused, so that the boy and girl are clearly pictured. The woman in the foreground is somewhat blurred and out of focus, heightening the ambiguity of her expression. She seems to be trying to overhear the conversation and may be on the verge of saying something. But nothing more is clear. Some kind of outcome is anticipated but cannot really be predicted. The picture has thus acquired a temporal dimension.

These examples should be sufficient to show the importance of the range of sharpness in photography. Since conditions vary from picture to picture, rules concerning its use cannot be easily formulated. However, the following observations are worth noting:

When all parts of a picture are sharply focused, the viewer can consider any part of it in much the same way as he would using normal vision. On the contrary, when the range of sharpness of a picture is reduced, his vision is unalterably restricted to seeing what is clearly focused. More limitations are imposed on the viewer.

Restriction of the range of sharpness is sometimes used to make pictured objects stand out. Thus, a close-up of a flower will be better if its natural environment is faded out. Excellent results from such close-ups can be obtained by using a telephoto lens and a sufficiently wide lens open-

ing. The entire environment of the flower is reinterpreted, composed as it is now only of more or less hazy splashes of color. Such a halo effect does not consciously attract attention, but tends to enhance the pictured object.

Objects or persons essential to the understanding of a picture may not be within the range of sharpness (as in the case of *Symbolical Photo* 531 above). In such a situation, the photographer does not intend to set them aside or fade them into the rest of the setting. Rather, by keeping them out of focus, he deliberately illustrates their ambiguous relationship with what is sharply focused.

d) Grain

Both the starkness and the simplicity of *Symbolical Photo* 507 are striking. Although perfectly sharp, this picture is almost a mere outline since the details are more suggested than clearly shown. The hands, for example, while expressive, do not show any apparent detail of skin texture. The emphasis, obviously is being placed on the total impression to be conveyed by the picture.

Among other things, this indicates that the quality of a picture is not determined only by the proper setting of the optical components of a camera. Chemical elements affected by light enter into play here, whether in films, plates, impression paper, or even cuts used for publications. The grain of a film can vary in texture.[7] The finer the grain, the more minutely the details of a picture will stand out. This is evident in the hand pictured in #22 of *Photolanguage*, "B" series.

---

[7]The light-reacting element of a film is usually a coating of silver oxide, granular in texture. The developing process will chemically fix those grains which have been more or less affected by light and free those that remain unaffected. In a developed film, dark or shadowy areas will be relatively free of fixed grains, while bright areas will show up as almost opaque. The actual purpose for which a film will be used and the developing it will receive will determine choice of grain size.

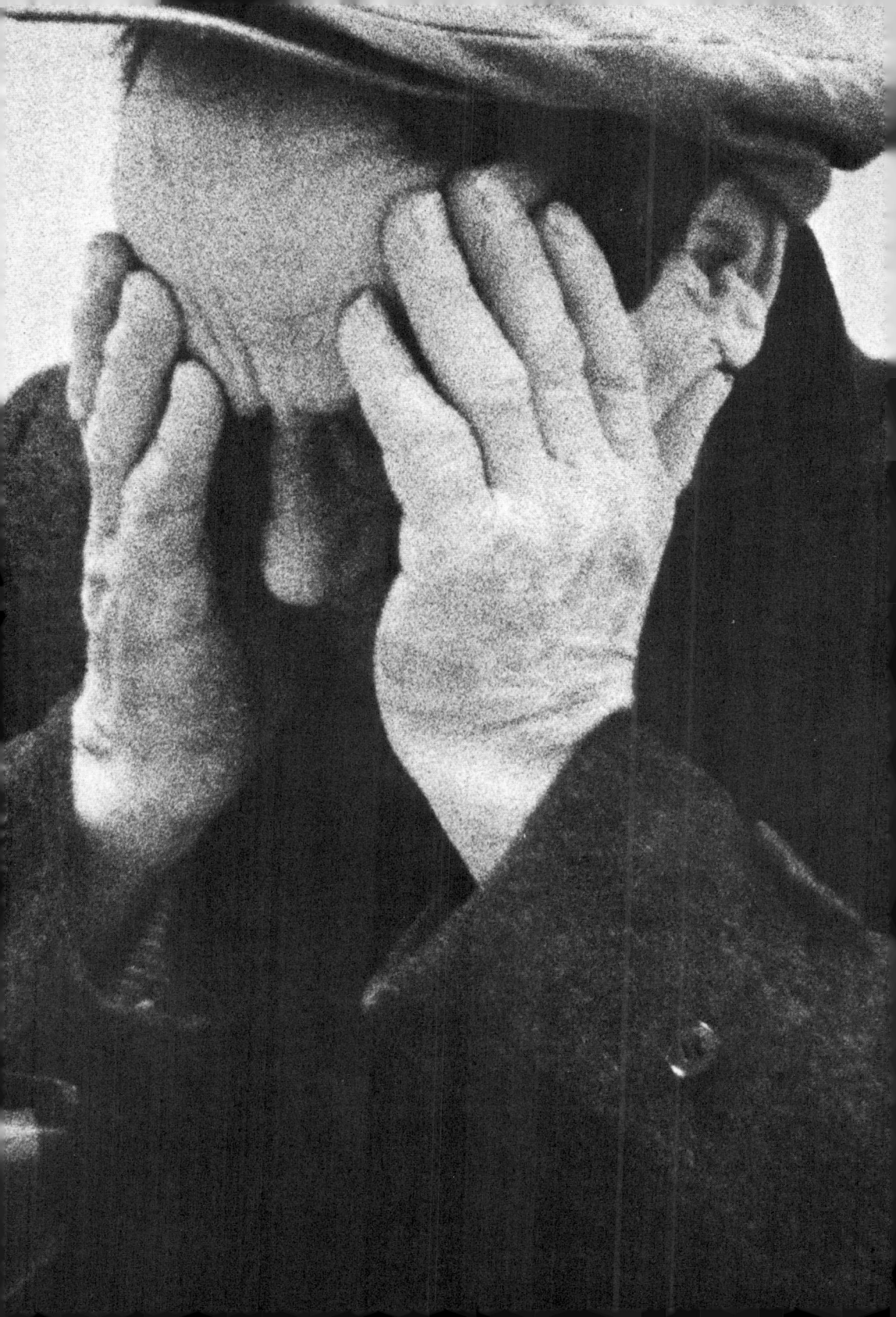

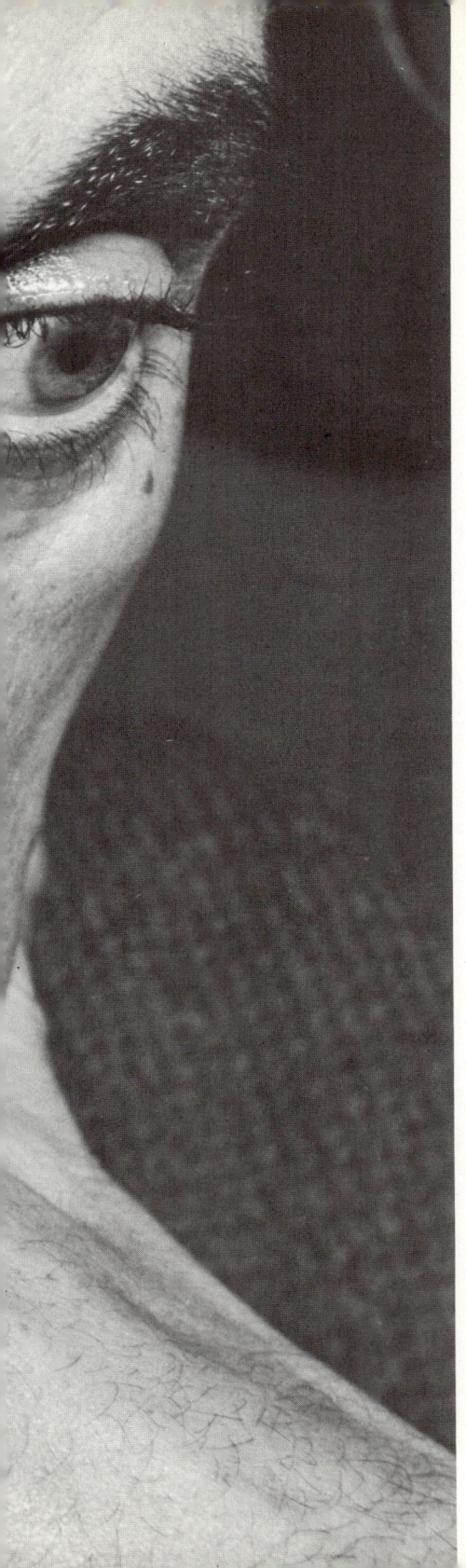

Fine grain stresses the realism of a picture. *Symbolical Photo 563* is a typical example. Everything in this almost frightening face is vividly realistic: every minute detail of the eye, every pore of the skin, every hair and whisker are pictures with startling accuracy. "What is truth?" says the caption. The very truth-value of this photograph illustrates powerfully the basic need for quality in pictures.

By contrast, *Symbolical Photo 557* has a dreamlike quality because of the rather coarse-grained film used. The picture has also been retouched: certain details have been brushed out and a halo effect has been added around the subjects pictured. Where the previous picture suggested durability and forcefulness, this one has a quality of fleeting transience.

e) Printing

Pictures are ordinarily printed on photographic paper. Slides can be duplicated. Professional movie film is copied before being marketed for projection. Each of the procedures is important, since the nuances of the picture and its color quality can be modified in the process.

Brightness and contrast, for example, can be given more or less emphasis in the printing of a black and white picture. In most cases, it is a matter of getting as accurate a picture as possible. This may require some compensation for the underexposure or overexposure of the negative.

Sometimes, however, special effects are desired. For example, a back-lighted subject lends itself easily to becoming a silhouette. Foreground shapes and details may be removed, even to the extent of obtaining, if desired, a picture with a cutout appearance. Generally speaking, these special effects will reinforce the aesthetic value of what is pictured, by either idealizing it or accentuating its dramatic impact.

2. The subjects chosen to be photographed

Vision is not a passive sense. In whatever it perceives, it recognizes familiar shapes and forms, interpreting areas of light, shadow, and color, and bringing them together to form objects that can be related to each other. These objects and their possible relationships are important, since they show the precise choices the photographer has made.

In the picture opposite, seven
men dressed alike, holding the
same tools, are at work. They are
lined up with such a similarity
of bodily attitudes that the meaning of what they do appears
basically identical. The neutral
setting is appropriate for the
group pictured. The picture is a
homogeneous whole.

The picture to the left is also homogeneous. In this picture of an ultramodern factory complex, shapes and sizes of buildings vary, but they blend together harmoniously. Their functional unity is also aesthetically pleasing.

As a matter of fact, these two pictures are, in reality, one. Together, they constitute *Symbolical Photo* 556, entitled "Two worlds." This is a typical case of contrast within one picture between two homogeneous wholes.

Such an example allows us to make the following observation: a picture is a complex of meaningful wholes. Each whole can also comprise a number of distinct subelements. A whole is homogeneous when its elements concur in giving it a unified meaning. Homogeneous wholes within the same picture can either complement or contrast one another.

Further comments concerning homogeneous unity:

A homogeneous whole is not necessarily destroyed by other elements in the photo. Such is the case in *Symbolical Photo* 560, where the wire fencing covers the entire picture.

The absence of discordant elements is required for a homogeneous picture. For example, at first sight there seems to be nothing amiss in *Symbolical Photo 539*: simply a well-dressed young woman in rather sophisticated surroundings. In all likelihood, the setting is that of a mountain chalet, suggested by the stonework and storm windows to keep out the intense cold. The entire scene evokes the peace and quiet of an evening spent in front of a crackling fireplace. One detail, however, is intriguing: the six half-empty glasses surrounding the girl. It then becomes evident that she is staring into space, as though lost in her own thoughts.

A picture can be quite homogeneous while being made up of disparate elements. The operating room of *Symbolical Photo* 526 comprises men, women, and a variety of instruments and other objects: yet, this is a unified whole. everything pictured has but one purpose: the success of the operation.

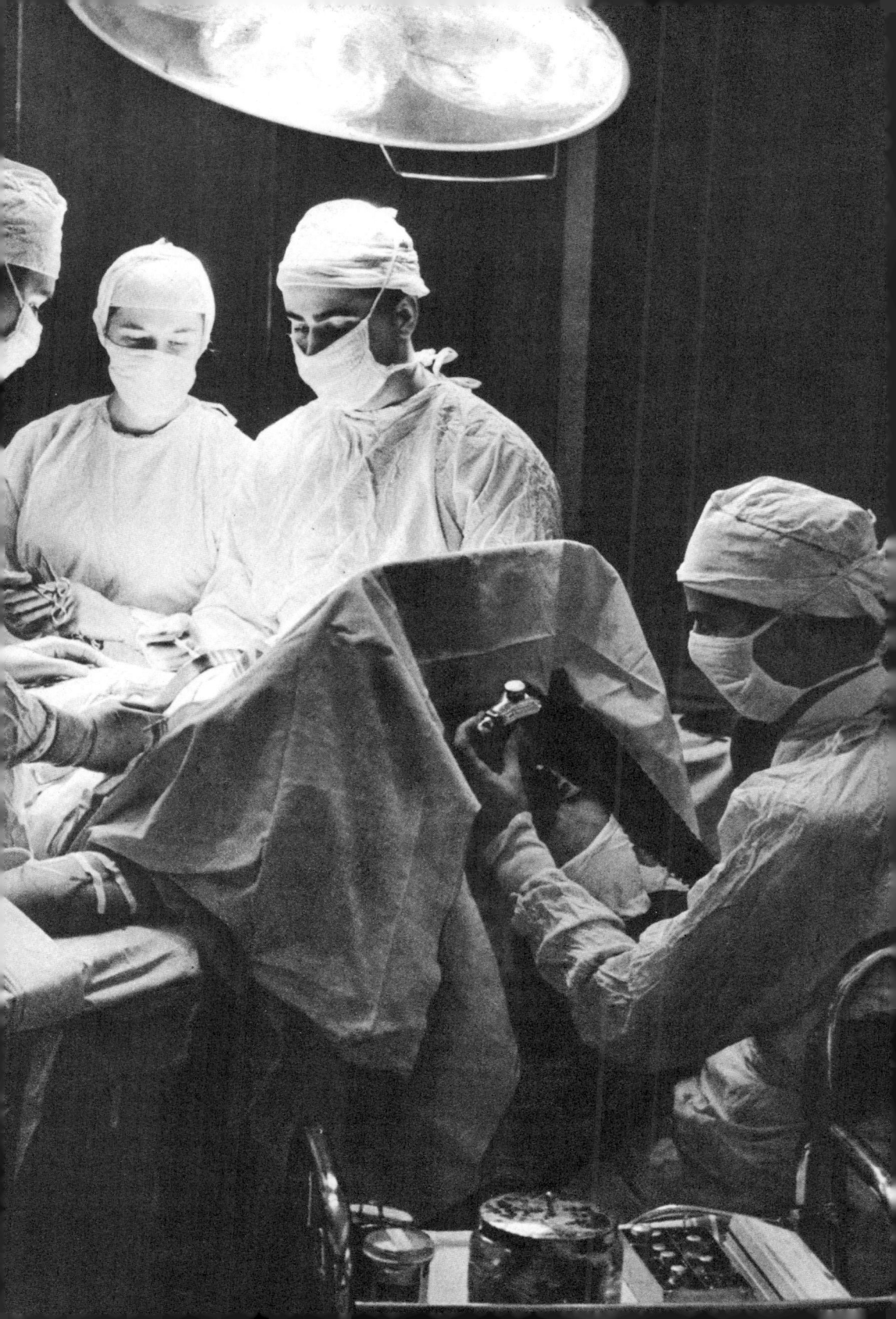

The aesthetic value of a picture
may reinforce its homogeneity.
Thus, for example, in *Symbolical
Photo* 516, men and boat form a
most eye-pleasing pyramid.

The setting or surroundings in a picture are by no means unimportant. It has been said, for example, that *Symbolical Photo* 543 is a perfect illustration of the vertical dimension of prayer, particularly Islamic prayer. In fact, the entire setting for the picture encourages such an interpretation. The vastness of the desert and the transcendence of a God found at journey's end still remain if the picture is framed in such a way as to include only the prostrate figure of the man in prayer (see opposite). But, the cliffs having been cut out of the picture, there remains no vertical dimension as such in the photograph.

The interest of a picture often
lies in the tension generated by
the juxtaposition of contrasting
elements. The picture above
is a portrait, nothing more.
The complete picture *Symbolical
Photo* 521, however, gives rise to
a multitude of problems: "In our
contemporary society, how does
a woman see men?"

The contrast of various elements of a picture can be underscored by their difference in size. Thus, in *Symbolical Photo* 532, the symmetrical unity of the radar antenna is broken by a workman's presence. Yet, the monstrous proportions of the reflector disk are accentuated by this intrusion.

E—SOME PRACTICAL NORMS FOR READING A PICTURE

Look for the total emotional impact of the picture

Absorb the complete picture, avoid focusing exclusively upon any of its elements. Blink your eyes to do this, if necessary. Let the total effect of the picture, and the atmosphere it creates in you, come to the surface.
It is on this level that you will become aware of the contrasts, impact, and basic nuances conveyed by the picture.

Look at the picture as conveying something that can be conceptualized

Look for the elements of reality being pictured, globally at first, then in detail.

Seek to conceptualize what is pictured. For example, the picture I am looking at could be replaced by the sentence: "A woman is feeding pigeons in the park."[8]

Look for the expressiveness of the picture

Examine not only facial expressions, but also the atmosphere created by the setting and the scenery. For example: a terrified mouse being chased by a monstrous cat, set against a rather neutral background.

Become aware of what the picture does to me

What does the picture do to me? What reactions, feelings, and thoughts does it arouse in me? Why?
For example, these comments from an elderly teacher: "I really identify with the old lady in *Photolanguage*, the one slumped in her chair, because her problem is mine. I am afraid of becoming rejected like her. Just thinking about it is terrifying. . . ."

Share with the group

Ask others to share their reactions, feelings, and thoughts concerning the picture. This will widen the possible subjective meanings of the picture and allow for a more objective reading of the picture.

---

[8] It is worth noting that such a conceptual analysis of a picture presents problems that stem from the mutual relationship of the objects being pictured. The resulting understanding of the picture could then be clear or vague. Examples:
A cat running after a mouse: the meaning is clear.
A cat and a dog sleeping side by side: the meaning is uncertain.
A dog sleeping in front of a plane: the conceptualization is so vague and ambiguous that it remains rather meaningless.

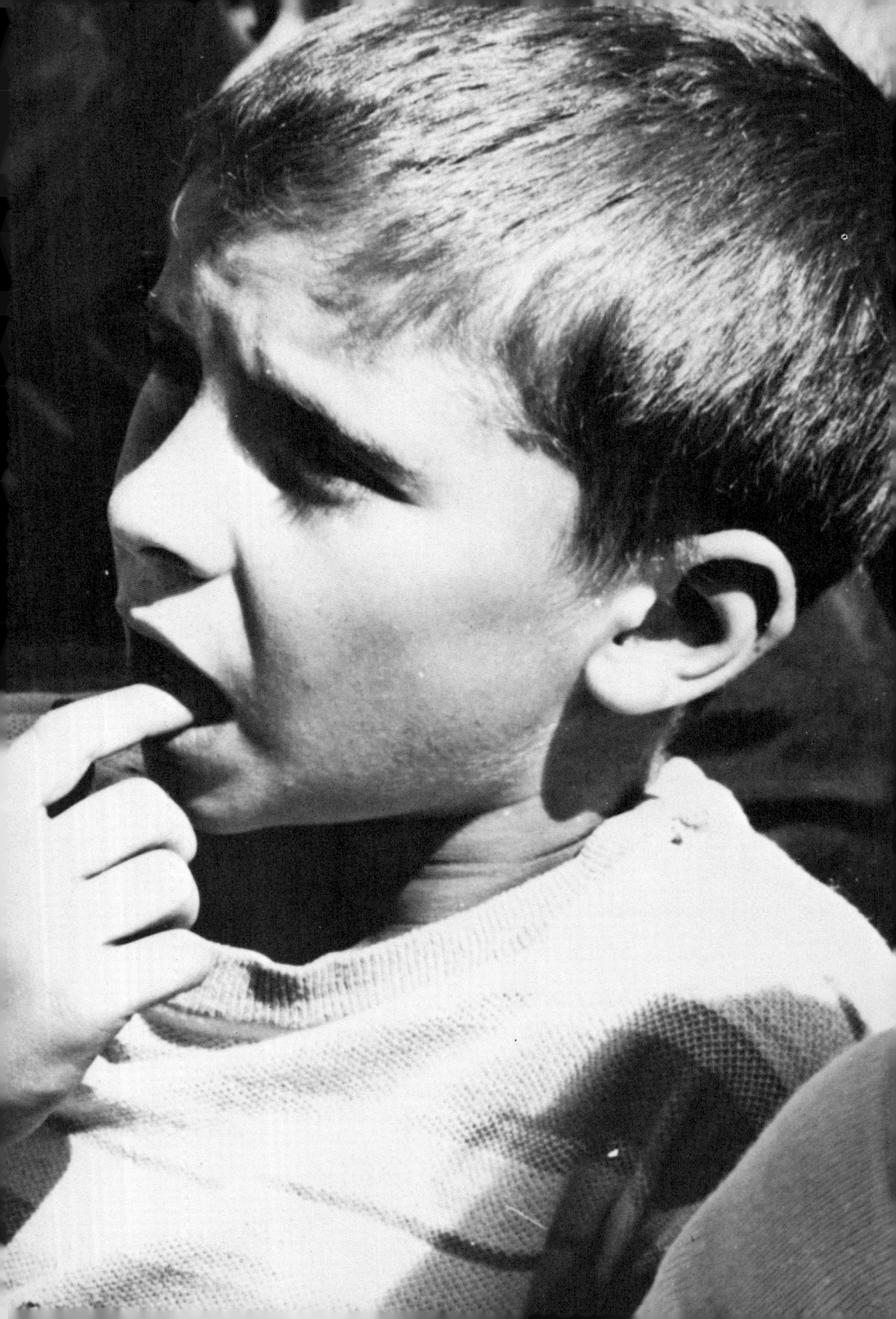

chapter 8

catechetical criteria

PIERRE BABIN

The relationships between sound-pictures and religion require clarification. Certain kinds of music and pictures are spontaneously associated with religion: organ music or magnificent panoramas for example. Similarly, certain actions, gestures, facial expressions, and voice tones evoke "religion." It sometimes happens, for example, that a priest driving his car and without any distinctive clerical dress will hear himself addressed by a policeman: "Father...." There is something about the way he looks or the way he acts that identifies him as a priest.

Different people have varying degrees of sensitivity to these associations. This sensitivity can be a natural gift or may be a result of training. Telephone operators, for example, whose sense of hearing is more developed than that of the average person, can recognize a social worker, a doctor, or the president of a company by his tone of voice and the way he speaks to people.

It is quite probable that the connections between sound-pictures and religion are valid only within a particular culture and within a given context. However, it is not enough to recognize this sociological dimension to religion. Even if we went so far as to claim that religion is a product of society,[1] we would still have to explain why it finds expression in certain soundpictures and not in others. Why are a certain tone of voice and a certain kind of picture associated with the religious dimension of life?

---

[1] Christians believe in a transcendence that is the source and form of religion: Revelation.

We have seen that audio-visual media is a language of its own and that it is capable of expressing the realities of faith. In this chapter we will attempt to describe which sound-pictures are religious and why this is so. To do this, two questions must be answered:

(1) Can sound pictures have a "religious" quality that would make them particularly apt for religious education?

(2) If so, how would this quality be described?

Can sounds and pictures have a religious character in themselves?

We must attempt to determine whether there is an objective relationship between a sound-picture and religious reality. To do so, we should distinguish two things:

(a) a religious document;

(b) a document that is apt for faith education.

This distinction is basic to the considerations of this chapter.

Religious documents

In certain pictures and works of music, such as paintings of the Last Supper or Handel's "Messiah," there is an objective connection with religion or with faith. In these cases, there is either an historical relationship that refers directly to religion, to Revelation or the Church, or the author himself expressly states his religious intention. A picture of Christ on the cross refers the viewer directly to a religious reality. To refuse to recognize a religious dimension in this case would be to disregard an objective fact. We can call this document "a religious document" in the same way as we can speak of a religious book store.

These pictures and sounds will be used very rarely in catechesis for adolescents.

In our present culture, these documents fail to evoke a profoundly religious or faith response. Young people have had too much of this kind of language during their childhood or at the beginning of their adolescent period. Everywhere this feeling of saturation is evident. "We're sick and tired of hearing about the Pope and the Bishops and the Council." "We've had enough holy things to last us a life time." "That song again!"[2] Pictures of this kind often appear **sentimental** (pastel colours in the St. Sulpice style) or **dated** (the works of the great masters) or essentially **illustrative** (pictures of Palestine). Young people are looking for a more powerful emotional language.[3]

Finally, in a secular age, it is of prime importance to help young people live their faith in the secular world. We have to help young people learn to see God in the world of men. If it is undeniable that associations we make as a result of our faith are gifts of God, it is also true that this faith must be educated and grow in the secular world. We can no longer live our faith in a "religious" civilization, as we did in the past when the formula was: we must bring religion into our lives. Because of the new sensitivity in our day and age, a more meaningful formula would be: we practice our faith by the quality of our lives.

Documents apt for a religious interpretation

We will not refer to pictures, songs, or sound documents as catechetical unless we are speak-

---

[2] According to the first results of a thesis on iconography under the direction of M. Tardy at the University of Strasbourg. M. Raymond Paquin writes: "Apparently the best reactions to iconography are at the age of 10; there is a maximum of interest, of acceptance of symbolism, and of concrete reactions."

[3] It must be added here, however, that some contemporary religious music can be very effective with young people.

ing of documents that are directly and intentionally "religious." To do otherwise would run a risk of distorting the documents. This has happened with the movie *Run* which has often been used in catechetical sessions and retreats for young people. The author, who is an unbeliever, did not for an instant see his document as a religious one: "I am stunned and offended by the fact that people ignore what I have tried to say and make me say something else. I attempted to bring out the crisis of western culture, not the spiritual anguish of a young man."

We distort a document by labeling it with an intention that was never in the mind of the author; to do this is to change the structure of the document and consequently miss its full meaning. A frequent case of this is the use of songs in catechetics. Even when we respect what the words say (and that is not always the case) we can easily change the emphasis. A song is above all rhyme, melody, and tone of voice; when we discuss with a group only the content of the song and its key phrases, we change its meaning. We establish as most important what is meant to be understood as part of an experience that is largely nonverbal. The whole thrust of the song lies in the fine shades of meaning this allows.

Even if we accept and respect this autonomy of secular documents, is it still possible to use them in religious education? We believe that these documents can be respected in their integrity and still be extremely valuable in religious education. This can be done by referring to these documents as being **apt for catechesis.** This terminology clarifies the issues and avoids giving an objective catechetical value to a document that does not have one. It simply recognizes a possibility, a certain depth or dimension that allows for catechetical development. After we have recognized the humanitarian and social meaning of the movie *Run,* we do not feel that we betray the film by saying that it is apt for catechesis or for further spiritual reflection.

What allows us to say that a document is apt for religious education?

Experimentation, and only experimentation. I can easily say that a certain picture of a girl is suitable for catechesis, but if my affirmation contradicts what happens in a group, I must question my evaluation. I can certainly continue saying that for me the picture is evocative, but I cannot say that the document as such has a strong positive value for catechesis inasmuch as catechesis is a group reality. Furthermore, only statistical experimentation—an experimentation that is frequently repeated, since cul-

154

tural contexts vary rapidly—can be considered as final. Otherwise we are speaking to ourselves, and the medium no longer constitutes a language since it fails to communicate.

It is true that even if no one recognizes it, an artist can create a painting that expresses an extraordinary message. Sometimes, the future proves that he was right—as with Van Gogh for example, and so many others. However, this is not the case in religious education. Catechesis must use a language that can speak and be understood today. Its ability to communicate today is an indispensable test of its catechetical value. Examples of some experimentation in this area are given as an Appendix to this chapter. The following points should be noticed:

(a) Preselection.
We must begin by a preliminary selection of the documents that seem to appear evocative. It is best if some educators as well as others who are knowledgeable about the nature of audio-visual language participate in this first selection. This saves time and avoids major errors in regard to good taste.

(b) Experimentation.
The purpose of this step is to discover the document's ability to gain and to hold attention, as well as its capacity to create a spiritual or religious reaction.

A document that has no shock value is of little use. Faith is awakened by Christ inasmuch as he is **"a stumbling block** for the revelation of many in Israel."

We cannot expect to arrive at the level of faith unless we have a document that is capable of shocking us into a new awareness and of challenging us to a new growth in freedom. Faith is not awakened by cliches or trivialities, nor by semiconscious perceptions. It is awakened only by strong and profound documents.

An example of a striking document with genuine shock effect is the picture of Che Guevara done in black and white shadows. Another would be the haughty and contemptuous young women in *Photolanguage* A-9 that one student stated "I can't stand." In other words, in testing the value of documents one should accept not only the documents or photos to which young people react positively, but also those they violently dislike. Evidently, one should avoid superficiality and the kind of sensationalism to which mass magazines seem to cater. The kind of shock value described here creates an impact that moves us deeply and forces us to think.

But shock value is not enough; the document must also allow the viewer to see some spiritual or religious implications. If most members of the group react to a central character by saying "He's funny," "He's drunk," or "Careful, he's going to fall," the spiritual value of this document is weak or completely absent. On the other hand, with a picture where all ties of railroad tracks seem to be crisscrossing (*Photolanguage* A-5) a large number of young people reacted by saying: "It makes me think of my future. I don't know where I'm going in life!" or "I'm moving, but will I ever get anywhere?" and again "Everybody's lost today!" It is impossible not to recognize here the recurring association of the railroad tracks with the deeper meaning of life. Certain documents even suggest a direct relationship to the Gospel: for example, when looking at the masks (*see Photolanguage* A-8), one group reacted by writing: "Whitened sepulchres, why do you always clean only the outside of the cup?"

Consequently, the essential quality of a document is its ability to provoke a spiritual reaction: its ability to refer people directly to Christian Revelation, or at least to the meanings of life. A document will be apt for catechesis to the extent that it has this kind of impact on young people, namely that it awakens in them a need to establish, to deepen and to clarify relationships between their life and the profound spiritual values of Revelation.

Photos Young People Like and Photos Apt for Religious Education

Young peoples' tastes are perhaps not those that readily lead to faith. In photos as in religious audio-visual montages, there is a gap between young people's spontaneous reactions and the world of faith. It is the same gap that separates the questions men ask about life from the new questions that Revelation introduces. Christ does not simply answer the questions men have been asking; rather he asks new questions. Francois Gonnet in *Documents-Service*, March, 1968[4] has attempted to determine the kinds of pictures young people prefer. The following are his findings from a group of young girls.

Nature: "The typical picture shows a herd of wild horses galloping in the sun. The movement in the picture evokes an impression of freedom. The grass is very green and in the background there is usually some very blue water and a glade of evergreens."

People: "Most of the time they are surrounded by nature: water, snow, or on a boat; a beautiful girl, her hair blowing in the wind, seated on the prow of a boat, with very blue water and waves coming up to her feet; she's looking into the distance and she looks happy."

Things: ". . . the interiors of buildings must have a great deal of colour, be pleasant and cozy . . . homes must be stylish and luxury items such as expensive automobiles are popular . . . Briefly, pictures must evoke something attractive: holidays, success, love. The technical qualities of the document do not seem to be important."

(c) Methods of experimentation

It is only with the whole document that experimentation is possible. We have no means at our disposal to verify the aptness of a sound or visual document in terms of elements that make it up (expression, contrast, melody, rhythm, theme, etc.) One even wonders whether it will ever be possible. It seems that there will always be the possibility of something in the document giving it an importance that hadn't been foreseen. For example, the picture of Cassius Clay (Photo Symboliques 505) will create certain reactions because he is well known in certain areas, or again the way a group reacts to a document dealing with death will depend upon whether there has been a death recently affecting a group. Consequently, the only valid way of experimenting is to evaluate the subjective reaction expressed by several groups of young people when they can react to the document as a whole.

---

[4]Gonnet, -*Documents-Service* (March 1968), P. 17.

158

The following are some of the questions that seem from our experience to be useful in determining the quality of a document.

1. Test questions dealing with the shock value of a photo.

Among fifteen photographs or an x number of songs, which ones do you prefer? Which ones do you least like? —Which photos (songs, music) seem difficult to understand? Which ones make you wonder about their meaning? —Underline descriptions in the following list that do not correspond to the document, and circle those that seem most suitable: happy — sad — dynamic — painful — peaceful — serious — indifferent — extraordinary — and so on.

2. Test questions dealing with the document's spiritual possibilities.

Give a caption or a title to the following photos. Express in one sentence your reaction to a song or to a piece of music.

Write down everything that goes through your mind after having seen or listened to a particular document. — Choose the three photos (or songs) that make you think.—-Record on tape the spontaneous reactions of a group confronted with the document.

In an area in which there are so many possible answers, the results should be interpreted by a group of competent and open-minded people.

II. What Qualities Make a Document Apt for Religious Education?

We can do no more than suggest the beginnings of an answer. These answers will evidently be debatable, but in an area that not been so little explored, we felt that it would be advantageous to try to establish at least an hypothesis in order to suggest and provoke more research. When an unbeliever, J. Letarte, a director for CBC T.V.[5] chooses posters and photos of artists for his Sunday morning televised Mass, the majority of the public including bishops find that they are very religious. One wonders why some documents have this quality. What type of sound or picture have "religious possibilities"?

Our hypothesis has two aspects:

1. A document is apt for religious education to the extent that it expresses a deep human situation which forces one to question the meaning of his life.

2. A document is apt for religious education to the extent that it expresses and promotes a spiritual exchange between the members of a group, when it allows them to share together on a spiritual level.

---

[5]See *infra,* chapter 10.

A deep human situation.

According to this aspect of our hypothesis, the qualification "religious" depends upon two qualities instrinsic to the document: the intensity, and the "spiritual meaning." Let us take for example the sound element. In a montage, the sound element is all the more evocative when it elicits **a reaction of our whole being to fundamental and profound values,** perhaps even in a violent way.

Accordingly, mood music, often played in airports and in large department stores, has very little religious potential. Its impact is very superficial. It does not move us deeply and we cannot commit ourselves to mediocrity and superficiality no matter how pleasant. The tone and melodies of mood music are not meant to move us profoundly or to awaken in us a deep need for a fuller life. On the contrary they lead us to buy things without much reflection, to recline on soft sofas, to escape real life in the decor of expensive restaurants. If we should pattern our lives according to this kind of music, we would not discover the religious dimension of life, we would not be open to something or someone beyond ourselves. One might go so far as to say that this kind of music anesthetizes rather than stimulates. On the other hand, Beethoven's Ninth Symphony or the music from "Hair" has a gripping effect. Such music makes us intensely aware of our deepest feelings and awakens within us profound emotions. This music is apt for religious education precisely because it makes us think and react deeply and forces us to break through the barriers of a humdrum and routine existence. In other words, it is the human depth and intensity that gives a religious character to a visual or sound document.

It is to be noted that the impact of sound depends less upon the content than upon the manner in which it is expressed. Boredom, for example, can be expressed in a trivial and superficial manner or in a way that is frightening and disturbing. The former is not apt for religious education because it encourages mediocrity; the latter, on the contrary, is very apt for religious education because it creates a deep reaction within the person that calls for a genuinely human response.

One wonders why a picture or sound has greater possibilities for religious education to the extent that it expresses what is deepest in man and awakens in us an interest in man himself.[6] Christians will find the reason for this in their understanding of what is "religious." For the Christians, something is religious if it expresses that "fullness of life" that is revealed to us in Christ.

---

[6]This is also true of great movies, for example Fellini's *La Strada* or Bergman's earlier films.

According to the Gospel, the Kingdom is open not to the rich, to those who are satisfied with the triviality of material wealth, but to the unsatisfied, to the violent, to those who would change our present social order. Thus audio-visual is all the more "religious" in that it appeals to man's need to become more human and expresses the depth, intensity, and violence that are the typical characteristics of the Kingdom.[7] To be "religious," audio-visual must conform to the words of the Gospel:

It is the violent who occupy
the Kingdom
I have come to bring fire
I have come that they may have
life in its fullness
Blessed are they who are hungry
and thirst
Blessed are they who weep.

We might say that if sound and pictures are to be religious, they must express those qualities incarnate in the person of Jesus: strength, depth, involvement, and an intense desire to live life fully, as opposed to dullness, triviality, superficiality, and evasion.[8]

What has been said of sound can also be said of pictures: their religious possibilities depend upon their dramatic intensity and their ability to portray the deeper meaning of life. A close-up that is accentuated by the use of fine grain paper, eyes that penetrate, or gestures that signify the human condition: all these are pictures that are most apt for religious education. They stir and awaken the viewer's conscience. In pictures, however, the objective dimension seems to be more important than in sound, largely because of the "personality" of pictures.[9]

A picture, by its very nature, has more content than sound. It is more like a definition and has a greater ability to express the mystery of life in a symbolic way.

---

[7] Intense human drama does not exclude humor and cartoons. What it does exclude is mediocrity. The extraordinary success of "Peanuts" is indicative of this. There is a tragic seriousness that may be technically intense, but humanly dull.

[8] All of this presupposes that Jesus is the "Revelation" of religion.

[9] Cf. chap. 7.

At the outset, it can be said that photos charged with symbolism[10] are most apt for religious education. Without delving further into the many theories regarding symbolism, we may give a practical definition of what we understand by a "symbolic" photo: symbolic pictures are those which evoke or reveal a meaning that goes beyond the mere image itself for a large number of people.

There are, then, two aspects which characterize a symbolical picture. First of all, there is a meaning dimension which suggests more than is materially present in the image itself. This "more" is a **meaning** that the viewer gives to the photo and which affects the viewer himself. For example, one can see in Che Guevara's eyes greatness, violence, and strength which disturb the viewer and stimulate him to action. The second factor that makes a photo symbolic is its ability to speak to many people. It is impossible to determine whether certain realities such as water are symbolical in themselves or only within a given culture. Pedagogically, we might say that a picture is symbolical when, in fact, a large number of people react to it in a spiritual or religious manner.

Pictures may be naturally or historically symbolical. A picture is naturally symbolical if the symbolism is relatively universal, as in the case of expressive hands or eyes. The symbolism is said to be historical if the meaning is related to a particular culture or historical event, such as an angry man behind the wheel of a car, or the atomic destruction of Hiroshima. Generally speaking, young people will prefer pictures having historical symbolism, probably because contemporary man no longer lives in unspoiled nature, but in surroundings transformed by man and his technology. It is not always easy to distinguish between these two kinds of symbolism. The photo of a man drinking in a bar may express the symbolism of wine that produces joy, or the historical symbolism of a man affected by that which a bar has come to represent in our culture. Only a close analysis of the picture and the usual reactions it provokes will allow us to determine what

[10]Since our concern here is essentially with the practical rather than the theoretical, we have used the expression "charged with symbolism" to avoid the enormously complex question of the real nature of a symbol. However, more study and research in this area are very necessary. Symbolism remains the key to understanding audio-visual language as a religious language. It would be necessary to study the symbolism in pictures as well as in sound and graphics. Cf. J. Colomb, *Le Service de l'Evangile,* pp. 410-418; 494-500.

Let us take an example of natural symbolism: I find myself in a semibarren, almost arid land near volcanic mountains. The sparse vegetation is bending under a strong wind across this seemingly endless expanse. I experience a need to run, to be free, to cry out, to make this land come alive. I am in a **symbolic situation.** The land is no longer simply the land near the Rocky Mountains, but something beyond this land, a kind of infinity without any definite limitations: freedom, the absolute death. Having felt this "spirit," I must now try to express it in a photograph, to record the connection between this land and the stirrings of my spirit. This is where artistic ability and technology enter: choosing the proper focus, the contrast of shadows, the play of light on the grass as the sun sets—all these are required to bring out the deeper significance of this land.

causes the symbolism: the natural act of drinking or the corruption of society "historically" evoked by the bar.

Whether they be naturally or historically symbolic, pictures have a capacity for relating material things to spiritual realities, and it is this power which constitutes symbolism. Herein lies the importance of these pictures in religious audio-visual material. A picture is all the more important religiously insofar as it is more pregnant with "possible meanings" for man.

In selecting pictures that will be apt for religious education one should look for symbolism. Through the use of techniques such as contrast, background, and viewing angles, these photos suggest a meaning, invite a response, or open up new possibilities for living life more fully. This requires above all that a photographer be sensitive to the "spirit" in objects and in situations, and this is an entirely different thing from merely seeing beautiful scenery.[11]

---

[11]A French critic speaks of the "dramatic moment." "By dramatic moment, I do not necessarily mean the most exciting moment, for example of a horse race. I mean the moment when something happens within you even if nothing happens outside you. Art consists in choosing this moment." This dramatic moment is what is called the "spirit" in objects, this "moment" in which we have seen a creature oppressed, hesitant, weak, *revealing possibilities not yet fulfilled.* This dramatic moment has a religious quality about it that relates life to something greater; this instant is the revelation of the openness of the human condition.

The presentation of basic human situations

Pictures that capture the typical situations or crises in which modern man finds himself (space travel, going to war, undergoing an operation, attending a meeting,) also have a symbolic value.[12] These situations represent fundamental human experiences for contemporary man. It is within these situations that he must fulfill his need to identify and to participate.[13] The best kind of photos for posing basic questions and suggesting religious realities are those which reflect these fundamental human situations in a way that brings out the genuine spiritual needs of man.[14]

Upon reflection, these situations appear as the contemporary equivalent of the major biblical situations in which the people of God encountered Him: Exodus, war, fear, exile, joy. By this very fact, they are privileged moments in which man is invited to exist either according to the Spirit or according to the Flesh.

The promotion of interpersonal communication on a spiritual level.

This is the second quality required of a document that will be apt for religious education. In determining an audio-visual document's possibilities for catechesis, we must not limit our consideration to the intrinsic quality of the document. It is also important to consider the environment or atmosphere in which the documents are to be used. This, of course, depends as much on the people involved as on the document under consideration. To be effective for catechesis, the document should create an atmosphere **favorable to interpersonal communication.** A photo will be effective in religious education to the extent to which it creates communication within the group.[15]

T.V. producers and directors are well aware that the quality of any production depends in large part on the quality of communication among the people involved in the production. Anger or nervousness will short-circuit a program. In preparing a televised Mass for his Canadian audience, producer J. Letarte [16] of CBC-TV considers the creation of a community atmosphere of prime importance.

---

[12]At Expo 67, Montreal, Canada, a number of these typical human situations kept recurring; they were photos with great human impact and meaning for men of our day.

[13]Friedman has shown that man gives a meaning to his life, not by abstract speculation, but by participating in and identifying with a particular crowd.

[14]These "fundamental human situations" have so many practical possibilities in catechesis that we have established an inventory and classification of them. See chapter 12.

[15]See chapter 9.

[16]See chapter 10, interview with J. Letarte.

Since the primary purpose of media is to encourage human communication, we may conclude that audio-visual catechesis has as its first objective the establishment of communication within the group. **An educator who does not use the media to create such communication is merely playing games with audio-visual material.**

Laws and Methods

In the first part of this chapter we pointed out the existence and significance of certain catechetical criteria, in the use of audio-visual material. Since this is so important, we should reflect further on some of the laws and methods that enable audio-visual materials to play an effective role in catechesis. The following observations are drawn from experience.

1) Using sound effectively:

Sound and music should be chosen in such a way that the important spiritual moments of a presentation are made more intense and more moving. These peak moments require particular attention if their significance is to penetrate the listener. For example, a long silence occurs as two eyes peer directly at the viewer, or a stirring melody or lyric rises to a crescendo during the peak moment of an action dramatized by a man watching a crowd from above. Rhythmic sounds, silence, or music may be used in creating suspense, an attitude of expectancy, an impression of moving toward something that will come — as for

Although not a Christian himself, Letarte has grasped this central understanding: it is impossible to create a religious liturgy without a group of participants who will interact and communicate with one another in a personal way. To be part of the group that creates the program in the studio is to enter into a relaxed and informal atmosphere which is at the same time fraternal and open. It is the quality of this communication which is largely responsible for the **religious climate.** The sounds and pictures amplify and focalize the interaction occurring within the group.

In this climate of communication amplified by the media, and even in the quality of the communication itself, there is a certain sense of the sacred, of a **Truth that requires a "state of grace with others."** Unless we share this presence, the sense of "being-with-others" is lacking; we feel excluded. We are reminded of the Gospel: "Where two or three of you are united in my name, I am among you." The presence of Christ, the experience of the "religious," becomes real each time Emmaus is reenacted in true sharing.

example, the sound of people marching. Sound that fills us with eager anticipation is spiritually significant; it recalls the words of God to Abraham, "Leave your country and come to a land I will show you."

Interviews of the voices of well-known people have great power of suggestion and realism. Martin Luther King's rhythmic speech "I have a dream" at the end of a presentation dealing with the racial problem in the U.S., or Helder Camara in one concerned with the third world, enables the witness to become present far more than a picture alone.

In order to make people think and to appeal to their conscience, we must not be afraid of using contrast in sound and music. Some kind of shock is often necessary. Above all we must strive for authenticity; there is an authenticity in sound that is very penetrating and disturbing. We have only to compare the authenticity of Joan Baez or Glen Yarborough with the theatrical formalism of Doris Day or Henry Belafonte and so many other popularized singers.

—Finally, only those recordings should be used that communicate an involvement of the speaker or singer. It should be possible to hear the emotion, the serenity, or the fear in the tone of their voices, in the way they breathe, in the vibrations or tranquility of their voice.

2) Pictures

For a picture to be stimulating, two laws appear important: mimic and contrast. Other important qualities must also be considered.

Mimic. Nothing appears more capable of opening up to profound realities than **man's own bodily expressions, such as gestures or facial expression.** In the words of Carl Dreyer,

Mimic is the elementary means of expressing psychological adventures and is more ancient than words....It is mimic which unites body and soul.

Regarding his film on Joan of Arc, produced in 1928, he writes:

I have tried to compose a hymn to the triumph of the soul over life .... We hope that our emotions may be aroused more by the development of inner conflicts than by external actions .... We cannot arrive at a true picture of man except through actors without make-up; this is the very essence of drama.[17]

[17]Retrospective on Carl Dreyer at Orly Airport, 1966.

We should give special care to close-ups in an audio-visual document, particularly to those of people. Such photos speak directly to one's conscience and solicit a personal response from the viewer. Close-ups are often the best way of ending a montage provided they include powerful and authentic expression.[18]

Contrasts. In audio-visual documents such as *Photolanguage,* contrast—a meeting of opposites —will be frequently used. It gives life and movement, it stimulates thought, and situates the problem. Contrast may be effected by presenting two pictures as antitheses or two homogeneous groups within the same picture, or again by opposing the picture and the text.

The contrast must explicate an anomaly, a paradox, or a real problem of which the viewer is already aware but only **implicitly and obscurely.** For example, the missionary problem: Should we still announce the Gospel to all creation? might be presented in the following way. On the right a picture of the President of Ghana saying on television: "Do not come and tell us 'this is right; this wrong!' We are old enough to decide for ourselves! If we make mistakes, they will be our mistakes." might be used; on the left, an African playing drums in church with the caption: "The Gospel has liberated us from the terror of the gods." Or to express the problem of the third world: the photo of a ragged child playing with a hoop near the shining wheel of a big American car.

Mood pictures and rare pictures. Some catechetical material for young people has been designed along the lines of popular magazines: a great deal of color and an abundance of photographs. Certainly, this makes the document more interesting and attractive. But is there anything catechetical about the use of these procedures? Have they any religious potential? Isn't this "commercializing religion"?

If we are to use this approach which is by its very nature a commercial one, we must assure ourselves that such an approach creates **a climate for catechesis.** It is not sufficient to create the kind of interest that leads us to leaf through the catechetical material as we would through a magazine, or to escape into the dream world of the movie magazines. We must not only create a superficial interest but a climate that leads to reflection.

---

[18]At the "Harlem on my Mind" Exhibit, Metropolitan Museum, N.Y. City, January, 1969, the last room was filled with close-ups of faces, mostly of Negroes with a few white faces interspersed throughout. All these eyes demanded an answer.

Finally, particularly when we are dealing with older adolescents and adults, we should choose those illustrations which lend themselves to reflection rather than to evasion and fantasy. We should not have too many "mood" pictures, but rather a predominance of strong pictures, a layout in which white areas, colors and shadowing invite silence and an awareness of self.

Symbolic photos. Photos that are most evocative of spiritual realities or of historical revelation are those that bring young people to see again a personal crisis, an anxiety, a strong desire or need that they are presently experiencing expressed in a visual document. A boy or a girl on a motorcycle can be a symbol of leave-taking, of the free life, of irresponsibility, or of love.

These photos or documents have a powerful impact on our life: it is important to find those that correspond to each age and **to each culture.** We should not try to avoid the **ambiguity** of these symbolical documents. Ambiguity is the test of a symbol and we have already indicated the degree to which symbolism is essential in evaluating the religious possibilities of audio-visual materials.

Illustrative photos or documents. Very little emphasis has been given in these pages to the use of documents as illustrations, since we do not consider these very important for adolescents, nor typical of audio-visual media. Unlike a younger child, an adolescent looks for moving experiences and rich symbolism. He is at an age that is particularly sensitive to symbolism. Consequently, he manifests a diminished interest in catechetical documents that are coldly objective. Although objective documents do have a place in catechetics, adolescents require more evocative documents to understand life. It is not antihistorical to insist that history should lead more to mystery than to science. It is in this sense that the Oriental Church has understood icons and relics. For the Orientals, to venerate a stone is not to be concerned about the historicity of the object, but rather to use our senses in communicating with what the stone recalls and evokes.

As a result, and particularly during adolescence, **evocative pictures** will have priority and we must see to it that historical or objective documents have a certain amount of suggestiveness about them. In this way a picture of Capharnaum could be nothing but a cold document, but it can also be a background that suggests a presence and a curse upon the stones.

The dead tree and the background remind us of Him who walked through this area saying:

"Woe unto thee! Not one stone will remain upon the other!"

Young people generally have been exposed to too many pious pictures and documents. This is an additional reason for using them rarely and for preferring documents which have a certain amount of shock value. We should prefer secular documents that are open to religious significance to those which are "pious". In these days of secular faith, to evangelize means to reveal the deeper meaning of all reality in the light of Jesus Christ.

THE MODELS
RACKET !

G

E THOUGHT
WAS GOING
A STAR !

Easy Prey For These
Merchants of Women!

THIS IS THEIR STORY-
THE TRUE STORY OF
THE MODELS RACKET!

I Don't Mind Going With These
Men If It Helps My Career-
But Thats As Far As It Goes !

PEDDLE THEIR LOOKS, THEIR
TALENTS AND THEMSELVES !

RL'S
ORPORATED

SHE'D STOP AT NOTHING
TO GET WHAT SHE
WANTED !

hard way...with the talent they think
the easy way... they co-operate

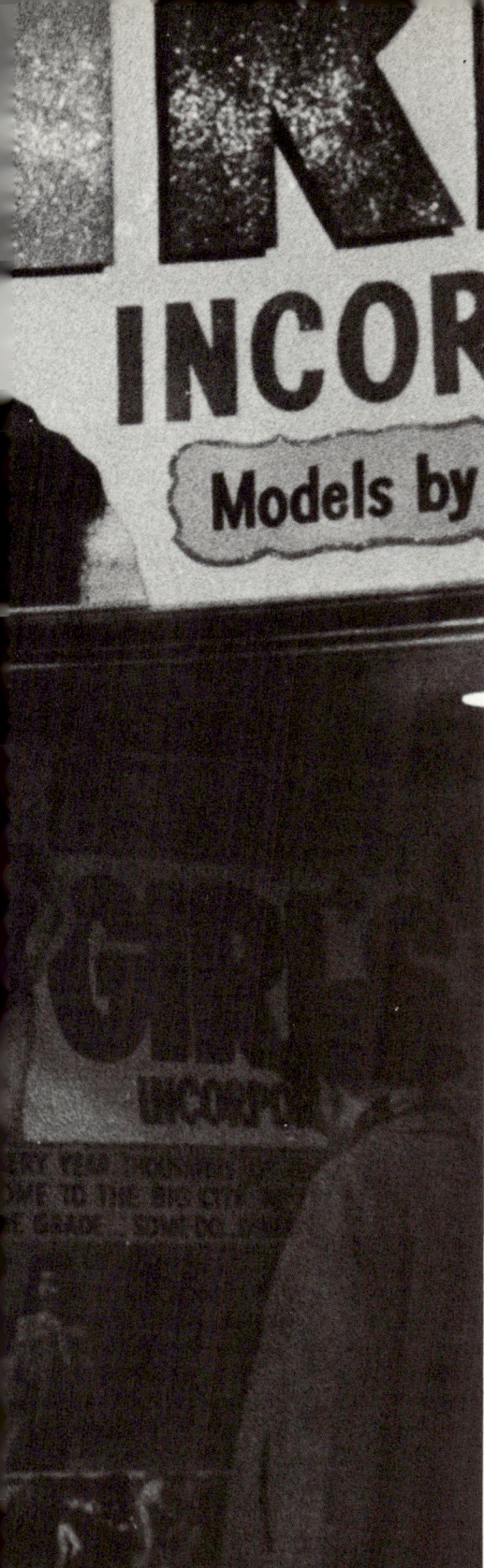

chapter 9

audio-visual
and the
creation
of community

J. P. BAGOT

Recognizing ambiguity

We are presently facing a revolution in the art of communication: electronic pictures and
sounds are replacing verbal communication. In fact, one questions the possibility of communication without the use of audio-
visual media in the future. But,
even though the impact of this
"new language'" is undeniable,
we must also be aware that like
any language it also has its limitations and ambiguities. It is
important for teachers and especially catechists to recognize and
understand this if they wish to
help young people communicate
with one another as well as with
God.

merely repeats what has already been seen. One has to come to a picture with an openness and a readiness to see and discover if it is to evoke a creative response.

Similarly, genuine audio-visual communication must avoid simply transmitting ideas already expressed verbally; it must communicate in a new form. Audio-visual communication requires creativity. It must transmit a world which in every way transcends explanation and conceptual interpretation.

Language, then, implies creation. What is involved in this creation? How can we be aware of the possible misunderstandings inherent in the creation of this new language?

Language that cannot be reduced to words

Contemporary linguistics has revolutionized our popular understanding of oral language. Language is really an organic entity having its own structural laws. Attempts to understand new forms of communication by simply transposing what we know about the spoken word are doomed to failure. It is impossible to transfer directly from one media to another. No dictionary translates pictures and sounds directly into words: we cannot move directly from the world of words to the world of sound and pictures. It is important to be aware that audio-visual communication is a new form of expression and that it has its own laws. It is not a straight translation of what might be said in words, but it simply opens up a new world of communication.

The organic dimension of forms of communication is evident in art.[1] Art is never art unless it creates its own form. While this is also true when one wants to use words in a new way, it is especially true of pictures. An exact repetition in pictorial language would betray the richness of the meaning. A picture is emptied of much of its meaning if it

---

[1] In his *Phenomenologie de la perception,* in which he analyzes the work of Cezanne, Merleau-Ponty describes the undefined perception that seeks expression within the artist. He points out that it is an indefinite but meaningful intention seeking to "become incarnate." But in order to express what he perceives, the artist is not content to use "ready-made" forms as we do in ordinary language. He cannot find satisfaction in "ready-made" meanings. "The meaningful intention is never anything else but the newness in my way of expressing what has already been said." The intention is fully perceived, however, only when it finds its form. In seeking a language, it reveals itself clearly. Self-possession, coinciding with oneself, transparency: these are not definitions of thought, but rather the result of expression.

THE FIRST AMBIGUITY

Audio-visual language must be understood as a dialogue between the communicator and the receiver.

The first ambiguity inherent in audio-visual language is also found in verbal communication. Both can condition one to be passive rather than creative. Language is creative dialogue when the receiver is actively involved in receiving the message.

Even in verbal communication, we cannot be merely passive in the reception of sound. When we hear a word, we do not simply record sounds, but we participate creatively in making them meaningful signs. Without this creative response, sound would remain mere noise. Sound alone cannot serve as a vehicle of meaning. We do not hear a language unless we can rethink it actively while it is being heard.

Audio-visual language is no exception to this rule. At first it may appear that it renders the listener even more passive. A certain color or sound might seem to evoke a purely passive response on the part of the receiver. Otherwise, mood music, for example would seem to manipulate people in much the same way as certain commercials which try to persuade the receiver without his even being aware of it. The point to be stressed here is that certain utilizations of audio-visual language reduce the activity on the part of the subject, even though this activity cannot be completely eliminated.[2] In such cases the ideal "receiver" is the one who doesn't consciously notice or evaluate the message he receives but is nonetheless consciously affected by it.

Advertisers don't seek to develop critical judgement in their viewers. If they did this, they would be encouraging a possible resistance to their product. The religious educator, however, must reject this manipulative use of audio-visual language. Unlike the advertiser, he must do all in his power to enable the recipients to become actively involved in the sound and images he presents.

---

[2]The slightest perception of color in the hearing of the most chaotic sound track is the result of a very complex activity on the part of the recipient. This activity is part of the process of human maturation. A newborn child cannot distinguish the various things in the world around him even though, from a physiological point of view, his ears and eyes are fully developed. It is through constant experimentation that visual space and sound gradually become organized.

All educators and especially catechists must be concerned with developing a critical sense within their students. They should also realize, however, that mass media culture like the former book culture, will have its casualties. In the past, there were always people who could not grasp the abstractions of the written word. There will continue to be people who are unable to grasp the meaning of concrete pictures and sounds properly. We must be aware of this if we wish to proclaim the Gospel to the people in a language they can understand. In no instance, however, should we merely condition the audience. This would be a betrayal of our very message.[3]

The danger of intellectualism must also be avoided. Audiovisual education does not result merely from discussion, because the inner meaning of any communication cannot be fully expressed in words. It includes learning the use of technical equipment as well as selecting and organizing of pictures, colors, and basic sound effects.

THE SECOND AMBIGUITY

Audio-visual education requires a shared experience

Verbal as well as audio-visual language can carry meaning as soon as one has personally mastered the medium. But this mastery will not in itself suffice to communicate meaning. For understanding to occur, the producer and the receiver must also

[3]A sympathetic critic of cinema, Jean Sullivan, warns about its dangers: Because Revelation is a mystery, intimate and secret, Jesus did not seek for publicity. If our apostolate does not avoid the methods of Madison Avenue, our entire system is illusory. It is not that these methods are intrinsically evil, but rather that in their present state when we apply them to spiritual realities they deny what they are supposed to announce. We have to go back to the whispered secret; we must substitute poverty, discretion, the Gospel in its purity, for the easy means of dominating masses.

It has been said that if Paul would return, he would be a reporter. It isn't true. His voice would be covered over by the incessant clamor of radios, the tons of paper that are dumped on doorsteps every morning. Unless he was gifted with a voice like Tino Rossi's or Gilbert Becaud's, a voice that reaches you "at the gut level," he wouldn't be heard, because the masses today no longer want to listen simply to hear someone talk; "they listen with their gut."

We have to return to the essentials. We cannot make pictures of God. Yahweh forbade the making of statues and pictures. Life is essentially interior. The most humble life is a beginning of consciousness, of spontaneity. Life is opposed to what appears on the surface.

(Plon, *Provocation*, pp. 84-85.)

share common experiences. Otherwise, there is no common ground, and the techniques of communication fail to stimulate a creative response and to become an effective means for interpersonal communication.

In considering verbal language, we tend to think that words and idiomatic expressions are of themselves meaningful to anyone provided the language itself has been mastered. Many think that words have a universally accepted meaning and that culture transmits to all its members precise rules of usage. In fact, however, **the meaning expressed by words is not automatic,** but rather the fruit of a subjective and therefore varying experience. Common terms like "gift" or "meal" are charged with meaning by those who use them or hear them — a meaning and content which are closely related to the life experience of each person. There is, of course, a minimal agreement upon their meaning, but the communication of the inner reality that transcends the materiality of a gift or of a meal is of another order. The life situations within which the words have been experienced affect their significance. One deciphers a message through his own personal code and although this code has elements in common with the code of other people, it nevertheless remains new and unique for each individual.

This law also applies to audio-visual communication. Even for those who have mastered the technical skills required for such communication, the ambiguities present in all interpersonal exchange are not magically removed. On the contrary, the difficulties of communication may be multiplied because the impact which the new form gives to the message may blind us to the necessity of the subjective response on the part of the receiver.

An educator, then, must not believe that the language he is using will have its effect **simply because of the technical competence of those with whom he is working.** Many people having mastered audio-visual language may be technically qualified to communicate with others through this medium. At the same time, however, their exchange may be impoverished because they are unable to imbue their common language with an inner meaning drawn from personal experience. In practice, we must be careful to avoid confusing audio-visual "activity" with communication. The mere use of audio-visual media does not ensure the communication of a spiritual message. This, of course, may not necessarily be due to poor pedagogy. It may happen that a particular class is very passive or that the young people have never known any real growth in their own lives because no one has ever challenged them to experience life. In such cases, communication fails because the message transmitted does not arouse and cannot arouse any deep resonance in the life experience of the person receiving it. At best it can evoke an unrealistic idealism without any impact on real life.

Take for example a meal presented audio-visually in order to bring out the significance of the Eucharistic symbols. Such a presentation could remain abstract if meals have lost their meaning in the everyday life of the perceiver. Only those who are capable of giving it meaning from their own life experience will react creatively.

Audio-visual education must actively involve the students or it will become as ineffective as any other form of education which fails to enter into a dialectical relationship with the lives of young people. Only lived activities can constitute an introduction into the world of signs, for only these activities can make people truly sensitive to meaning.

One cannot enter into the world of cinematographic or photographic communication and at the same time remain closed to the everyday communication expressed by a bowl of flowers lovingly arranged or a meal prepared in a special way by a loved one. Such a person's dialogue with

the world by means of technical knowhow would be illusory. Even his photography would reveal his superficiality. Technology may allow us to see more, but it does not automatically increase meaningful perception. It can only be helpful when it is used by people already tuned in to life.

The need for group experiences:

These considerations lead us to conclude that the use of audio-visuals is most effective as a group experience. All human beings share some common life experiences. In the same way, any group shares certain specific life experiences simply because they are participants in the same group situation. But these common experiences are often very superficial. Even when they have some depth, their capacity for creating bonds within the group often goes unrecognized. In such a situation it is difficult for the educator to create a community within the group. His first task, therefore, is to lay the groundwork for communication. Even in purely verbal exchange, the educational value is greatly increased when the group has shared a meaningful experience. In any group involved in a common project, certain words become loaded with meaning for all the members. Certain allusions can be understood immediately.

The repercussions of such a shared experience are just as great when audio-visual media are used. **Such an experience gives signs an affective or emotional impact.** A picture can acquire a wealth of meaning; sounds can recall common experiences. When a group of people who have become a community see their own experience reflected audio-visually, it becomes a language that evokes a creative response from them. Audio-visual language can then be the medium for communicating a very meaningful experience. This makes it apt for the expression of religious values. Throughout the presentation, the group reviews what it has just experienced and perceives in it a spiritual significance.

On this level, communication can take place even without words. Pictures and sounds have become vehicles of revelation. They are "parables" because they have been penetrated by a dynamism that springs from the common life experience. The inner meaning of the group experience is revealed.

Group Experiments in Religious Pedagogy

Although the experiments described here did not take place within a school situation, teachers familiar with the use of group techniques may find them adaptable to classroom use.

Two groups of boys at a summer camp undertook a recreational building project: one group built a small fort complete with observation tower, while the other set up an Indian teepee. For many, it was the first time they had ever handled tools and they found a great deal of satisfaction in what they had accomplished. A team of the boys then prepared the Eucharist for the end of the day. After a great deal of discussion, they decided to organize the liturgy around the notion of building. Certain biblical themes suggested by the chaplain led them to agree on the following themes:

"A human building is always fragile if it is not supported by a solid family. Our God is a God who has promised to build a solid dwelling, which is the Church, the community of those who believe."

All were aware that their fortress and their teepee had taken shape only after each group had overcome certain difficulties. The young people who had the responsibility of organizing the liturgy began to recognize, however, that what they themselves had understood only after a great deal of thought and reflection could not be communicated to the others by words alone. They needed some kind of visual presentation.

At the entrance to the room in which the Mass was to be celebrated, the group placed pictures of the buildings they had just completed. Beneath the illustrations were the words: "We have built ourselves a house; unless you come and live in it, it will soon crumble."

All those who participated as well as those who had planned the ceremonies were deeply impressed by the association of the pictures of their work with the Eucharist. Everyday life had now become a sign with a meaning for the present as well as a challenge for the future.

In a similar situation, pictures of what had been built were accompanied by the projection of slides indicating building projects that are taking place in the world. A picture of the U.N. indicated the efforts men are putting into changing our world. In this way, the experience of what had happened in a small group was associated with the problems in the world. The faith message acquired a more universal and profound meaning.

In yet another situation a group of teens returning from a game was carrying on a lively discussion about the various aspects of the game. "Who really deserved to win?" they wanted to know. The dynamics of competitive sports are important to the growth of young people. It would be wrong to reject sports, games or contests on the pretext that they create conflict. Yet, one must lead young people to see things with more perspective to help them understand that fighting it out is not an end in itself. Here again, this can be illustrated by the juxtaposition of pictures.

One group chose six photos and presented them to the others. Three photos represented fights between young people during some sports events. Above these three were placed a picture of Ian Paisley and one of Bernadette Devlin, key figures in the crisis in Northern Ireland occurring at the time. Above these was a picture of Ghandi with the inscription: "Who won?" This experience took place on Wednesday in Holy Week. The text of Isaia read: "He was despised and we took no account of him . . . . Yet through his wounds we are healed" (Is. 53: 3,5). The reading of the Passion comes to commemorate the apparent "defeat" of Christ, a defeat that ended in triumph. No sermon was necessary. Their own situation was dramatized. The pictures situate the real question; the meaning of Scripture is clear. The Eucharist itself takes on new meaning: the commemoration of a victory.

"Say it with flowers"

The following experience took place with a number of young adults during a session on group leadership. The experience is far richer than the preceding ones but the approach is much the same: a number of people come together as a group by learning to share common experiences and in doing so they must overcome the difficulties people face when they wish to create a community. In a second stage, symbolic figures and pictures permit the group to see as though in a mirror the evolution through which it has grown and become a community. This also allows a deepening of the experience by associating it with the outside world, brought into the situation through pictures.

This is how it happened. The first three or four days of the session were marked by confusion and futile search. Recognizing the difficulties the participants were having in coming together as a group, the leaders of the session had asked whether they could learn anything from the recent assassination of Martin Luther King. The majority of the members had simply answered that King meant very little to the children for whom they were responsible. The chaplain then illustrated the meaning of the question by carrying a revolver to every session. In reaction to the astonishment of the members, he explained: "It may be of use. When a group refuses to face its problems, there is always a time when it picks up a gun to eliminate the people whose questions disturb them. I want to be able to defend myself when you reach that stage." As the young people gradually grew into communities, they realized how group tensions lead to aggressiveness and violence when they are not faced honestly. The awareness of the difficulties in creating a group made them realize the meaning of their efforts: they were solving on a small scale problems which are not always solved in larger groups. Through the positive use of nonviolent or "political" action, they were able to confront and thereby eliminate those tensions which lead to assassinations, either actual or figurative, within any group. They had learned to make assassinations obsolete.

Throughout the session, a large room had been used for meetings of the whole group. At the beginning of the session, someone had suggested that it be rearranged, but the groups were not yet capable of doing that. They had not yet realized community in a sufficient way for any rearrangement to be an expression of the group. But on the last day of the session, the chaplain and one of the leaders had spent the morning rearranging this room. They selected those words which had become important during the session as a way of describing the growth of each group, using symbols and pictures to express them. Each group could then see an image of its own growth and could recognize a religious meaning in their experience. The altar arranged for liturgy, was the center towards which all the representations and symbols converged.

At the end of the final morning, the participants asked the chaplain for a session on religious pedagogy, that they themselves might better understand their role as Christian educators. To their surprise he replied: "After the three hours I spent with you this morning, such a session would be useless. I have nothing to add." "But we didn't see you," they objected. "Probably because you didn't know where to look," he replied.

At the end of the session, the participants found themselves facing a picture of Martin Luther King in the common room. Below it was a gun; behind it, a bouquet of flowers seemed to bud forth from broken glass, barbed wire and thistles. Written above the picture was a phrase from a song written by Gilbert Becaud: "The olive tree will flower again." At the entrance to the hall, a banner announced: "I have something to say to you. Will you hear me?" "What have you to say to me? Say it with flowers." In this way the meaning of Easter today was proclaimed in a visible sign. It symbolized the whole session; it illuminated their world made present by the picture. The picture itself reflected the real meaning and significance of the whole session.

On the altar, the bible was open at the Gospel of the day. When one of the students began to read, the whole group discovered a new meaning to words they had heard many times before: "Their hearts had been closed . . . they did not recognize him . . . their hearts opened up and they recognized him at the breaking of the bread" (See Luke 24).

The evening celebration began with a wide-ranging debate that made use of A.V. media. The song "Who Will Answer?"[4] now took on a new meaning. One group selected two slides from a number they had made: one was a ray of light, the other a loaf of bread broken into pieces. These projections now took on new significance as they became an expression of the group's experience. The pictures represented how the groups saw themselves, as well as a plan for their world. They were now ready to celebrate the liturgy of the Eucharist.

---

[4]Ed Ames: "Who Will Answer?" RCA Victor.

Conclusions:

It follows from the above illustrations that an image becomes a very powerful symbol insofar as it expresses the dynamics of a group.

The picture itself may be taken from some other context. It achieves importance when it transcends its individual value and becomes part of the group interaction. It then enables the group to become aware of what it is experiencing. It can in that way constitute a privileged means of announcing a spiritual or religious message.

To discover its religious meaning, the picture must be related to the Word of God. Announcing the Christian message, however, can be something very simple. In some instances, religious words can be entirely superfluous: a series of circumstances can of themselves link the Gospel to a picture. The Gospel can have more impact when expressed visually than when announced verbally. Because it stimulates one's creative imagination, a picture can provoke a far richer response than words. Silence can contain the Word of God; it is this Word in the picture that makes us open to another dimension, one which transcends human experience. Only for those who know the meaning that Jesus gave to his life and to the Last Supper does

it make sense to combine a picture of Martin Luther King, a gun, and the altar. For him who lives the Gospel, it is not necessary to verbalize this meaning: it is the "Word" that revivifies what is visible.

The picture has a further advantage. It respects the freedom of each member of the group. Words and sentences have very precise and limited meanings. Some may be comfortable with these, whereas others have more difficulty in finding their experiences expressed in the spoken word. Pictures, however, open up an unlimited horizon; they avoid giving a special meaning or importance to an expression that is relatively limited. Each person sees his own discoveries in a graphic manner at the same time as he finds himself in communication with others who also see the picture as personally meaningful.

When it springs from an experience that has been shared by a group, the language of pictures offers a means of communication that transcends words. Through pictures, intellectual as well as nonintellectual people can communicate.

This kind of visual pedagogy presupposes a change in the mentality of the teachers. They must surrender the "security" which requires that they know ahead of time what must be said and how they will say it. They must on each occasion be open to the experience as it happens and discover in it the language of that experience and the signs that can express it. Audio-visual media come in at a second stage facilitating real dialogue with the students.

Used in this way, audio-visual language will avoid the reproach that is so often made against it, namely, that it is capable only of introducing people to material products. It will become, on the contrary, an authentic means of participation. By giving free play to the imagination, it will enable people and groups to experience the appeal that comes from a transcendent, which from the beginning has manifested itself to man by inviting him to dream of horizons far more vast than those of everyday life.

PART III

**projects
and
projections**

chapter 10

audio-visuals: dream or reality?

Pierre BABIN interviews J. LETARTE, producer-director of "Le huitieme jour," a weekly presentation of the Sunday mass by Radio-Canada (the French network of the Canadian Broadcasting Corporation).

Throughout this book, the underlying question has been: Where will audio-visuals lead us?

In January, 1969, I participated in a televised mass produced in Montreal by Radio Canada. Afterwards, I had a lengthy interview with the program's producer, J. Letarte. Not a christian himself, he spoke simply, honestly, and enthusiastically, as a man—as an audio-visual man.

Personal reactions to the approach used may be favorable or highly critical. However, it is important to realize the tremendous potentials of the techniques used and proposed by Mr. Letarte.

The pages which follow are both an invitation and a question.

189

A professional

BABIN: How do you see your role as producer-director of the Sunday program?

LETARTE: I am a **professional.** . . . It may appear pretentious to affirm this from the outset; but I **am** a professional. Consequently, I deal with the religious program "Le huitieme jour" in the same way as with any program I produce or direct.

Choice of theme

My text is the current Sunday mass. Before doing anything else, I first read the mass texts. The theme I will use arises from these readings. Once I have found the theme, I must fully explore it. This week, for instance, everything pointed to children. So I studied the child from all angles: the serious child, the joyful child, the child in his daily activities. Therefore, during the mass, we had children going to school, children playing, eating, children living out their child-role fully, that is, living out their role of "potential young adults."

Development of the theme

BABIN: Where do get your ideas for theme development?

LETARTE: This requires a certain sensitivity to the texts and also and in-depth awareness of human experience. Let us say that is requires that the producer have a certain capacity for research. Returning to the example of the children—in my opinion it is not necessary that we talk about children as "christians-to-be," or see them performing "devotions." I find this irritating. A child who breaks a window acts like a child—and this is how I portray him. This is the child I want to speak of during the mass. I draw extensively upon my own experience of children when developing this theme.

BABIN: Once you have found your theme, do you think in terms of pictures or writing?

LETARTE: My background as a painter leads me to think pictorially; I then translate these pictures electronically, using the technical means most suitable to give them greater impact. A multiple-screen system and 35mm slides are particularly effective. By projecting pictures from many sources onto one screen, film-type continuity can be created. The use of close-ups enables me to isolate and frame those elements I want to emphasize.

My dream is someday to have a technique which allows projection in space without the need for a screen.

The script

BABIN: In preparing your program, do you work from a precise script?

LETARTE: No. I have developed a chart which divides the mass into approximately thirty parts. For each part, several possibilities are provided for, rather than a final choice made in advance. For example, I foresee ten to twelve possibilities for both the gospel and epistle readings. To illustrate what I mean — this morning I had expected the epistle to be read loudly and firmly. As it turned out however, the reader was soft-spoken and somewhat reserved. This necessitated choosing an alternate picture that corresponded more closely to the quality of his voice: the picture could not be vibrant when the delivery of the text was weak. I had a complementary picture at hand. We must prepare for many such eventualities.

BABIN: This program must then require tremendous preparation.

LETARTE: Yes, it does . . . . For the mass, I do everything from memory, having seen and read the texts so many times. Still, someone quipped the other day that the program is called "The Eighth Day" because a week is insufficient time to get every-thing prepared! However, the technicians and I are not alone in preparing this program. The participating community also helps out, and the celebrant, Father G. Dubuc, is of tremendous assistance. He is the one who, at times, prevents us from making foolish mistakes.

Sound: song and music

LETARTE: The congregation is composed of working-class people having no special degree of culture. What they do possess, however, is the desire to sing and to pray together. We gather every Wednesday night and discuss the theme of the mass for the coming week and the songs that would be suitable. But the musical arrangements are completely original. These are all prepared and prerecorded for the Sunday telecast by the choir director. We could easily publish many of these masses.

BABIN: Why do you create a new musical theme each time?

LETARTE: Because we have to keep in mind that the mass texts change. Of course, after a while, some of these musical themes recur.

BABIN: What kind of accompaniment do you use?

LETARTE: The music we use is increasingly electronic. We have kept very few traditional instruments except for percussion, piano and guitar. We use an electric organ, an electronic harpsichord, as well as electronic guitars. We have not yet been able to develop electronic percussion instruments, but this will come; there already are possibilities in using the microphone itself as one. The accompaniment varies with the themes. One week we might use three instruments, the next, ten. We experiment with instruments continually. For example this morning the guitarist discovered new sounds by placing plastic inserts between the strings. Now we compose new music to incorporate these new sounds.

Settings

Stage props are plastic so that the congregation's view will not be obstructed. All the sets are variable in size and asymmetrical. We have even chosen uncomfortable chairs so that people will be forced to move! They must not be passive spectators.

The role of the producer

BABIN: What are the producer's responsibilities during the program?

LETARTE: He selects the pictures, makes the choice of lens to be used, supervises the movement and placement of the camera equipment, and gives the signals to start or stop the music. I keep in constant touch with the technicians by interphone. I can thus reach thirty to forty of them constantly, giving information,

suggestions, and encouragement. Sound-mixing, however, I leave to the technician who is by my side and follows my hands more than my words. He follows my gestured instructions much like a musician responds to the baton of an orchestra director. However I do place the cameras and supervise the composition of each of the pictures myself. In directing picture selection, I use electronics a great deal, as well as a multiplicity of other instruments. For example, let us say that I call for an expressive profile. My technical assistants find it for me. Then I restructure the picture as I really want it, asking that it be reproduced, for example: "20% white, 80% black," "Lengthened face," and so on....

The congregation

BABIN: Up to this point we have talked about the technical aspects of production. But what does your "audience" do? What is its role?

LETARTE: Perhaps you noticed that in our studio no one coughs, or clears his throat, or blows his nose. This is an atmosphere that we do not want disrupted. I have seen people leaving the room to cough in the hallway. In the churches, there is this sort of intense silence during the consecration, but when this part of the mass is over, people relax.

Here, the people are caught up in the climate that has been generated. Once, a fire started near the candles suspended to the ceiling, and hot wax was dripping down. No one noticed it except the one it fell on, although there were five hundred people present that day. Another time, the theme of the mass was human suffering; reference was made to the situation in Biafra, and some people actually had tears in their eyes. At times, the climate is so stimulating that children spontaneously speak out, and people clap their hands.

Sometimes, after mass, people comment: "How will we ever go back to our parishes and take part in the masses there after an experience like this?" Others have remarked: "It requires a certain state of grace to belong to this group." And this is exactly what happens: we are built anew, renewed by the group. The results are remarkable. We discuss the theme before the mass and again at the end. These discussions are noticeably different, mainly because some very extraordinary things happen during the mass.

Let me illustrate this. This morning, my five-year old son was at mass. Since, in his words, "dad makes the mass," he began to sing. At communion time, when he saw the congregation moving forward, he said: "I'm going too. Everyone else is eating, I want some too." But a woman stopped him very gently and said: "You are too young." Had it not been for this woman he would have received, although he is only five and not baptized. In my view, the spontaneity of this child's gesture should not have been cut short. He was participating! Later, he went around asking everyone: "What does it taste like? Do you like it? Is it good?"

You should also see how we "empty" the hospitals on Sunday: from 10:30 to 11:30 A.M., during the program, there is no one around the wards. Almost everyone on staff is watching the telecast. A Protestant pastor has even asked to belong to "my" congregation.

These things make you stop and ask: "What is happening here?" This mass is a gesture of men, a gesture expressing a tradition, but using a medium which happily has not yet become habitual. These people can be said to be virgin soil, and this is an asset. It is up to us to provide a good presentation. And, believe me, they are changing; they are becoming an adult community.

For a mass that is virile and genuine

BABIN: You are not a Catholic. How did you become interested in this Sunday mass program?

LETARTE: This telecast is closely connected with my personal history. Last summer, I was producing one of the most popular programs in Canada: *Fleur d'amour, fleur d'amitie* (Flower of love, flower of friendship). Every day, 10 to 15 thousand people came to the *Plateau*,[1] where it was being produced. One day, I collapsed, totally exhausted from overwork. After a stay at the hospital, I was told that I needed rest and less demanding work. To find such a task, I turned to my T.V. set, and tried to choose the most conventional program I could find, the one most easily produced. And I found the weekly televised mass—nothing was more conventional than the T.V. masses I saw. They were merely the telecasting of what appeared to be a boring ceremony. At the time, I thought that this was the job for me—it would only take two days a week to do something worthwhile with this program. When I arrived at the studio, I read the mass texts and said to myself: "Why should the program be so poor? These texts are very beautiful. I really must do something about it!" I then devised the fomula with which I am now experimenting.

BABIN: Does the way some priests celebrate mass sometimes annoy you?

LETARTE: Well, when gestures, such as genuflections, have no interest for me, I simply eliminate them. I do the same with certain texts: some are irrelevant to modern man. On the other hand, however, there are certain things that cannot be changed in the Liturgy of the Word or of the Eucharist. These are traditions that I respect, just as I would respect the rules of the game in televising a particular sporting event. Whether I agree or not is of little importance.

But, when a priest says: "This is my body, this is my blood," he believes in it even though I don't. Therefore, when he says it to me as though he were stating some commonplace things such as: "Go out fishing; it will do you good," or "Who hasn't seen the Rockies?" what he really deserves is a good swift kick! If he believes, he should be aware that he is making a human gesture of extraordinary value. He is given an opportunity, in his faith, to produce a miracle. Consequently, he should communicate it in the virile manner it merits.This is the essence of my task, and it is for this that I will always strive: I want this mass to be made into an experience that is virile in the true sense of the word—virile in the sense of "manly"—expressing man's power and strength, and excluding all affectation. I am interested in the presence of

[1]The *Plateau* is one of Montreal's better auditoriums, and telecasts involving large numbers or extensive audience participation often originate there.

man, in the presence of God: but it is the role of the priest and congregation to contribute to the latter. And I believe that television, because of its mysterious, "miraculous" qualities, renders this possible.

Let me use another example. One day, at the moment of consecration, my son asked me: "What the priest is doing now, is it magic?" Such words are childish, but they underscore an important reality. By concentrating the lighting on the central action, by supporting it with background music and pictures on the screen, I had succeeded in giving him an inkling that we had arrived at a moment of mystery. It is in this way that we can also lead adults to this sense of mystery which has been so overlooked in our churches.

The future

BABIN: How do you envision the future?

LETARTE: Thanks to piles of mail and hundreds of phone calls, we have come to realize that many, many people are watching the Sunday T.V. mass and regret not being able to participate. So we have decided to use a number of churches for each weekly telecast.

The procedure is a fairly simple one. The music and slides to be used in the parishes are prepared and sent out two weeks ahead of time. All the participating churches have the same slides, songs, and accompaniment. At 10:30, before the mass, a discussion on the theme of the day originates from the main studio, with feedback coming from each participating parish. This simple expedient enables us to pick out the congregation that is most responsive; more than likely, we will choose to broadcast the mass from that parish. In any case, discussion from any of the participating churches can be fed back to the main studio, which then acts as an anchor desk. After discussion, all participate in their own parish mass. The singing could originate from the parish church or be broadcast from the studio, according to the producer's choice. After the liturgy, the discussion on the theme of the mass can again be resumed, adding to it now the experience that has been lived in each individual parish.

Such a procedure enables us to reach three to four hundred parishes. The next step could easily be a telecast originating from and beamed to all parts of the globe. I would really like to cooperate with Paris, London, the major cities in the U.S.A. We would then be dealing not with 400 possibilities, but with 50 million. . . . This would surely be a worthwhile undertaking.

I would also like to see the Pope taking part in this mass—not in a conventional way, but participating in a mass for young people, either as celebrant or deacon or even only as a singer. This would be marvelous! This is what Christ came to do: He didn't come for any other purpose than to be a man, the "super" man . . . and to participate on the same level as others. How do we know this? When he realized he had to die, he had the normal reaction—he became afraid as others do.

I am fortunate to be here, where faith in man is a reality. Moreover, with television, we are starting to think not only "horizontally" but "vertically" as well. As a favorite proverb of mine goes: "It is better to be stiff-necked from looking up than to be hunch-backed from looking down." Where faith in man is strong, people experience a need to talk with their God. This is what makes these televised masses meaningful for me!

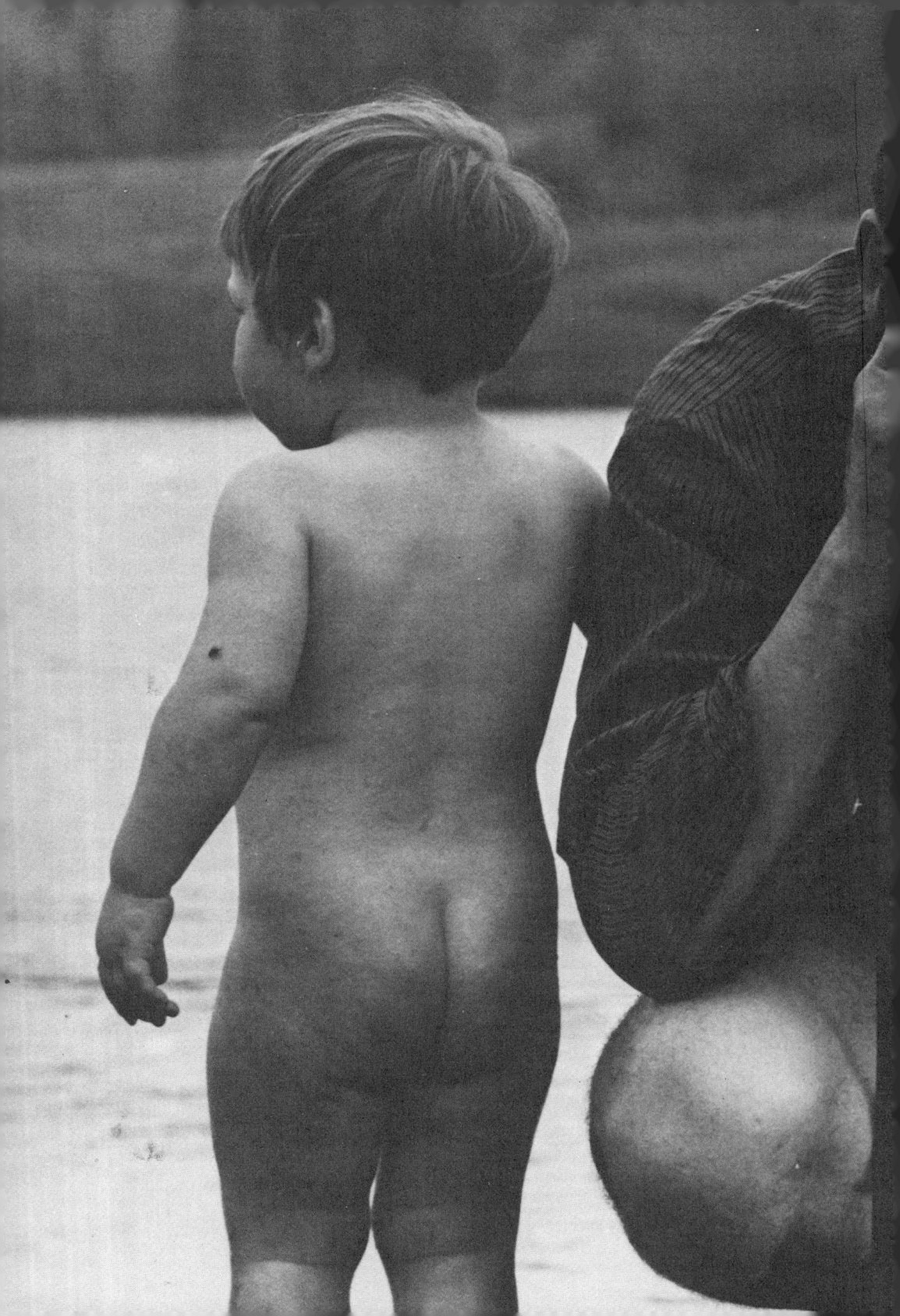

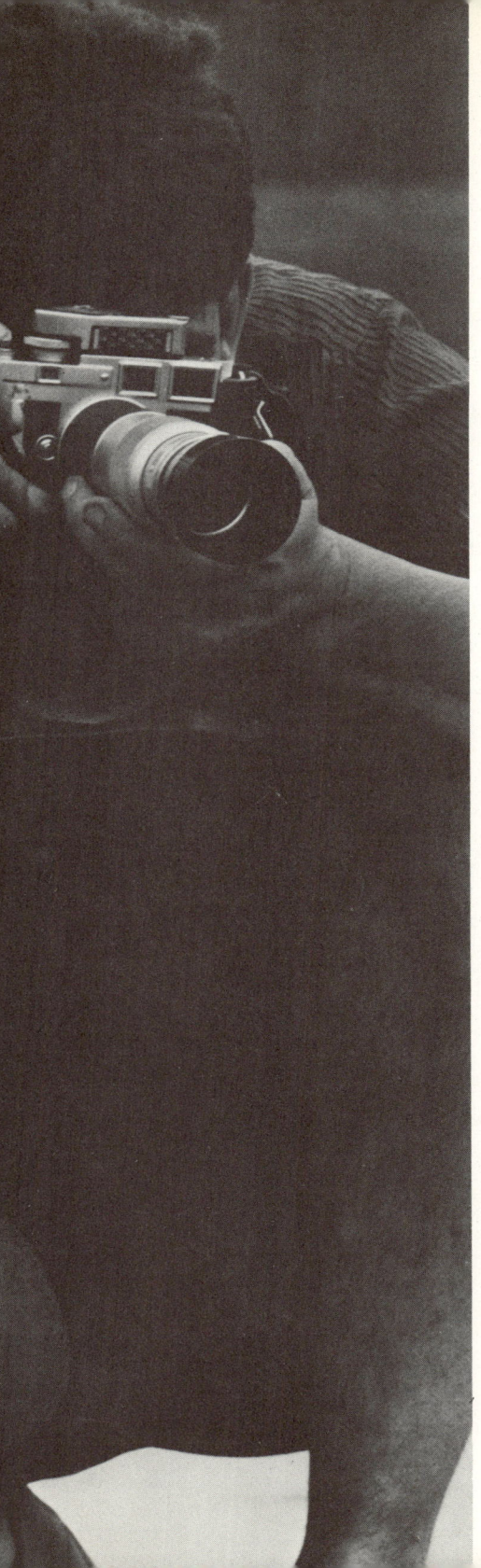

chapter 11

guidelines for beginners

PIERRE BABIN
CLAIRE BELISLE

Where do we start?

Educators often say: "We're convinced of the necessity for this new language, but how do we go about it? The world in which we grew up was so different. . . ." Those who wish to leave the "Gutenberg galaxy" and discover the new world of audio-visual media will find here concrete suggestions as to how this can be done. Some assistance in educating young people in audio-visual language will also be given.

This chapter will deal first with initiation into audio-visual language, and secondly with the use of audio-visual equipment in the creation of montages. A third step, the art of film-making, which adds movement to the above combinations, will scarcely concern the majority of religious educators, and is therefore beyond the scope of this book.

As in all audio-visual usage in catechesis, the educator must keep in mind that he is constantly involved in two operations: one of faith, and one of critical evaluation. An ability to go beyond the obvious and to discover the deeper spiritual or religious significance of reality and to express it effectively are indispensable conditions for the use of audio-visual media in catechesis. This kind of penetration and readaptation, however, is only possible through frequent critical evaluation and reflection, not only on audio-visual documents but also on life and the Gospel.

LEARNING THE BASIC ELEMENTS OF A-V LANGUAGE

1. Learning to see:

Looking at very good pictures is one of the best ways to develop a photographic eye. Become critical of the photographs around you. Compare them with award-winning photographs. Ask yourself why a particular picture received an award. Study the composition, the angles, the interplay of light and shadow. Find out what in the photograph is suggestive, evocative: "What is the photographer saying? How does he say it?"

2. Learning to use a camera:

To photograph is to learn to see, to select and emphasize; it is learning to say something with pictures. This technical training is important if we are to see and speak audio-visually. We must always be careful to avoid the conventional-type photography found in family albums.

Start, therefore, by seeing, that is by selecting, by noticing contrasts. Become aware of the background, the foreground. Organize the setting to really bring out your subject. Always ask yourself: "What do I want to say?" Bring out what is typical of something, or someone: a gesture, a mimic, an action. Try to capture that fleeting instant when things "come alive."[1]

Be alert to those realities and scenes which are typical of man, his worries, his miseries, and his hopes. Search for the human element. For example, in the hallway of an old house, I see about fifteen mail boxes, some new and still shiny, others broken and partly torn from the wall, some made of carefully varnished wood, others of rusted metal. . . . They almost seem alive for me. I need then to find what angle, what lighting will be needed to express best what these mailboxes say to me about their owners.

---

[1]For the technical aspects of this section, consult any good photography book or manual.

Examine the streets like a reporter or a press photographer would, always on the alert for contrasts, for striking details, for everything which provides new insights or sheds new light on old facts.[2]

Work with young people; get them to express a particular theme in photos, posters, brochures. Experiment with pictures: try to tell a story, to convey a message, to express a personal idea.[3]

3. Learning to hear:

Learning to hear is not easy: we need to be convinced from the start that noise, silence, and music are not only an auditory background for the word, but constitute a language having its own importance and meaning. The following points in learning to hear should be stressed:

Listen to descriptive or contemporary music. This type of music is probably more important for audio-visual language than its classical counterpart, since it strives to amplify and interpret present-day life.

Make a note of the images and feelings that accompany such music. Try at least once what some ardent lovers of descriptive music advocate: listen to it in the dark, at full volume. Go to a concert of contemporary music; feel the atmosphere and listen to the reactions around you.

Try to isolate sounds with a tape recorder. A sound can be picked up, accentuated, detached from a background, amplified, depending upon what you want it to

signify. For example, you could isolate the noise of a soldier on watch; his step is very typical, it has a certain fullness, a particular heaviness and rhythm. It speaks of something that is slow and steady: it creates an expectation. Experiment by building up a story with sound only, and then have others listen to it to see if they understand what you wanted to say.

Try to recognize the sounds that are usually associated with a particular situation or state of mind. Thus the chimes of the Westminster Tower clock ringing the half hour suggest that something routine and regular is happening.

Pay attention to the music, the moments of silence, and the sound effects used in films. How are they combined? What is the purpose and effect of the silent moments? Silence in a film is not to be considered as an emptiness, but as a positive and extremely significant moment. Musical themes in films are important: notice when they are repeated and why. Those who listen to weekly TV programs such as *Mannix* know that certain melodies or special themes announce or underscore the climactic moments.

---

[2]The art of reporting involves finding a new angle from which to present information the public already knows.

[3]See *Photolanguage* (Ottawa: The Catholic Centre of St. Paul University, 1969, and Dayton, Ohio: Pflaum).

As many different kinds of technical equipment as possible should be used in learning how to master the use of audio-visuals. Through the use of equipment one learns to select, to amplify, to correct—and consequently, to communicate. Is this not the highest use of technology?

4. Initiating young people into audio-visual language:

Young people also need to learn to see and hear. Very often, audio-visual techniques appear to them not as an in-depth language, but as a superficial yet enjoyable way of expression. They are not accustomed to seeing such media used seriously, and consequently think educators are only trying, in a more pleasant way, to make them swallow the "pill" of the Word. They will take reading or listening to the Bible seriously, as well as discussion about it; but not looking at and discussing pictures. Consequently they must be helped to see films, photographs and records as part of a new language, of an amplified language. At times, it will be necessary to begin with the ABCs of audio-visual education: analyze a picture with them, listen to a record, teach them how to "see" through the eye of a camera.

Young people must be taught to experience the artistic quality and the evocative power of good audio-visual documents as fully as possible. Mere technical mastery of audio-visual techniques is not sufficient for catechesis.

Young people must learn to see, hear, and feel the deeper dimensions of human experiences. They must be awakened to the unsuspected spiritual dimensions of any human situation: to learn to see hidden worry, desire, and fear, to recognize the call for help in an outstretched hand or in tear-filled eyes, and perhaps even to perceive through these signs the mystery of Him who is the "heart" of man. Is this not one way in which we as educators can, within the dimensions of secularity, fulfill our role to make the blind see and the deaf hear? Certainly we are called upon today as Christian educators to help man develop the deepest dimensions of his existence.

LEARNING TO CREATE AUDIO-VISUAL MONTAGES

The next step is to learn how to combine pictures, music, sound effects, and words in original montages. Entire series of pictures can be prepared in advance in projector slide trays. Sound tracks comprising music, sound effects, and spoken text add a further dimension to the visual element. Ideally, the students themselves should help to create the montages.

1. Models

High quality commercial montages should serve as models for new creations; they enable us to recognize good script and the basic relationships between picture, sound, and word. Analyze how in advertising the interaction between music, sound effects, and voice communicates a single message. The study of televised newscasts, documentaries and programs such as "The 21st Century" will also be useful.

2. Script

The first stage of a montage is the writing of the script. This is a particularly important and exacting stage. Your script will have catechetical quality and depth only if you have something relevant to say and are saying it effectively. Too many montages have no catechetical value —not even human value—because they are empty words, illustrations, and sounds amounting to meaningless jargon. A montage must express a desire to communicate, and presupposes that you have something to say and a clear idea of what this message is to be.[4]

For the drafting of the script, the page may be divided into three parts: TEXT—SLIDES—SOUND.

Time-cues may be added to indicate precisely when slides are to be changed. At first, the various parts should be put together in a tentative way. As the montage takes shape, criticize your text, your choice of slides and sound effects in order to make the whole more coherent and concise. At each stage, ask yourself: "What do I want to say through this picture, this sound? Is it meaningful? Where do I want to focus attention?"

3. Evaluating a montage

Ask other educators to criticize your work. Have them indicate its strengths and weaknesses, as well as the sections which are too lengthy, or lacking in interest or smoothness.

It is in working with the equipment at hand that you learn how to convey your message through it. There is a sort of man-machine covenant that can only be achieved when a man decides to work with a machine. At times, the technical equipment itself

---

[4]Too frequently we become amateurishly preoccupied with the technicalities of a montage and neglect the content. Combining pictures and sound for which one has a feeling can be interesting for the one who is doing it, but unless the audience and the message are clearly kept in mind, we may end up talking to ourselves. In order to communicate, a genuine poet not only welcomes inspiration, but masters his language as well. Avoiding abstract intellectualism does not remove the burden of having something to say and knowing how to say it.

will give new possibilities to your expression: for example, the echo effect of certain tape recorders or the overlay in the Veronese projector. On the other hand, the equipment will frequently place limits on what you want to say. Yet you can only speak within the limited possibilities of the tools you use. To overwork an instrument is as artificial and annoying as to force one's voice.

INITIATION INTO THE CATECHETICAL ASPECT

It is essential that audio-visual language be mastered, but there is more to audio-visual catechesis than this. What does initiation into the catechetical dimension of audio-visual language require? There are two dimensions—one of faith and one of critical evaluation—which must always be kept in mind.

The faith-dimension

The primary requisite of an audio-visual catechesis is that it originate from someone who believes, who has something to say, who feels deeply within himself an urge to proclaim the hidden treasure of the Gospel. Otherwise, the audio-visual media will remain a "gimmick," a "cover" used to speak surreptitiously of a Christ whom we find dull and uninteresting. On the contrary it is essential that Jesus Christ be the "supremely interesting person" of whom we gladly speak. To express this in journalistic terms; we must have a message to give, a message we consider of utmost importance. For religious educators, this message is the Gospel; it is faith that brings new life.

But how can this message, this "point of view" that comes from faith be translated into audio-visual language? Look at the human realities in faith: see men, things, and situations in the light of faith so as to discover their spiritual dimensions, the connections with the "fundamental reality" revealed by Jesus Christ. Secondly, try to express this dimension, not by spoken or written words only, but by combining sounds, pictures, and words.

Where and how can we begin? It is impossible to give a "recipe." The "seventh sense" that faith gives, the "prophetic vision" cannot stem from any magic formula. The following suggestions will provide some assistance. Their value lies in the fact that they have been drawn from practical experience.

1. Immerse yourself in the audio-visual world

Choose high-quality films, tapes, and LPs. Search for profound and intense audio-visual experiences, since depth and intensity lead to emotions of a spiritual nature. This does not mean looking only for the great masters, or for well-established actors and producers. As a matter of fact, the latest films of Bergman and Hitchcock, for example, appear more artificial and stereotyped than earlier productions; also, while the early Belafonte was sincere, his latest recordings seem more formal—you feel the technique rather than the man. What is important is to choose only what is authentic and unaffected.

2. Pray with audio-visual media

Do not hesitate to pray with a beautiful picture, to take the time to contemplate the inspiring pictures of such magazines as *Camera,* or to listen prayerfully to the latest LPs. Bring the modern musical idiom into masses for young people as much as possible. Encourage them to create their own expression of meditation, of communion, with guitars, slides, songs, and pictures.

3. Find pictures, sounds, and melodies which foster a sense of wonder, peace, and openness

Try to discover what aspects of revelation are suggested by different pictures and sounds. For example, to initiate students into the language of pictures, a catechist asked them to choose, from among a large number of photos of everyday life, those which could express the life of Jesus Christ. For many, this activity was a real revelation: forced to look at the photographs intensely and in depth, they gradually experienced how certain pictures recalled specific phrases of the Gospel, making these "come alive" with contemporary meaning.

Faith means choosing and emphasizing certain aspects of reality; it is seeing in depth, seeing a new way; it is establishing links between different dimensions of reality. Audio-visual language enables us to accomplish this more effectively than does the printed word.

4. Group communication

In Israel it was customary for prophets to live in groups. Undoubtedly, they enabled each other to see more clearly and to take a stand on vital issues. Also, Teresa of Avila danced and played castanets with her community of nuns to express her love for God. In group life, we have one of the great laws of initiation into prophetic vision. Audio-visual media can play an important role in creating this group spirit. It should be remembered that the spiritual potential of audio-visuals is closely related to a spirit of openness and sharing among the members of a group.

Looking at reality in a spiritual way and linking it with the Gospel does not belong to the sphere of dogma. Just as you can't limit the meaning or dimensions that Simon and Garfunkel give to street lamps in "Sounds of Silence," so neither can you exhaust the spiritual significance of daily life situations. It is sufficient however that someone sée and hear with great intensity in order to stimulate others to see better and with greater depth. A prophet always gives rise to other prophets: his mode of action is not to impose, but to awaken, to stimulate, and to suggest. To discuss a film with people who think deeply, to communicate one's own reactions to advertisements, to share what you see in a photograph or the meanings that we see in situations and events: all this is essential for initiation into a prophetic way of looking at the realities of our time.

One thing still holds true: nothing can take the place of personal reflection, meditation on life and on the Gospel, with a constant correlation of the one and the other. Group communication really bears its fruit when it is enriched with the reactions and the reflection of at least some in the group.

Critical evaluation

For those who have not grown up with audio-visual language, its mastery requires more than a simple introduction to its various elements. A stranger cannot know a new country unless he incarnate himself in it, and become conscious of how different it is from his native country; so it is with those who leave the "Gutenberg Galaxy" to enter into the realm of modern audio-visual media. They must immerse themselves in the world of audio-visuals, but they must also regularly and constantly reflect, compare, and look at things from different perspectives.

The greatest temptation for adults is to see audio-visuals as mere distractions. TV is an evening narcotic for those who are tired; the radio is a relaxing background—a cigarette for the tensions of daily life. When this is so, the impact of audio-visuals is lost. Audio-visuals, which could have been a new and powerful language, become merely hypnotic. Instead of being media for communication, they become obstacles to it. Therefore, the necessity of experimentation, of analysis and systematic reflection concerning them cannot be overstressed.

While the reading of books on audio-visual initiation or on the sociology of communications may be highly useful, nevertheless nothing can replace a constant self-questioning. Experience proves that the best way to know something is to measure its effects, first upon oneself, and then upon others. For example, after listening attentively to a recording of percussion music, I ask myself: "How has this music affected me? What mood has it created? Have I become more anxious, more relaxed, strengthened, more open?" Sometimes—without forcing the issue—questions that are more spiritual will come easily: "What words of Christ could I place in this context and why?" Other questions will stem from the group: "What reactions do others have to this record? Why is it that people often either feel annoyed or fail to react when they first hear an electronic recording?"[6]

CONCLUSION

One further consideration should be added here: audio-visual language and the ability to use it well is not something that happens suddenly. It needs to be assimilated by our body, by our nervous system, by our whole person. As has already been pointed out, a driver does not feel his car as part of himself from the very first time he slides behind the wheel. And so it is with audio-visuals: in a year or two we may discover that we have become "totally other," that we do not speak as we did formerly.

---

[6]Becoming aware of the possibilities, advantages, and limits of the audio-visual language is all the more important when one has the responsibility of being an educator. On October 12, 1955, Pius XII went so far as to say:
Will this ever-continuing technical progress keep alive, perhaps, the unrest that assails not a few contemporaries by the increasing dominion of technology and its application? Will it perhaps happen that its extraordinary advance and expansion will subject man even more to the power and the dominion of material processes up to the point of removing him from his natural and legitimate position of master and arbitrator of reality? Without doubt, this thought merits serious consideration; nevertheless we believe that every harmful influence upon the dignity of the person can be warded off provided technology, like any other temporal good, remains always in the first place at the service of the soul, of spiritual ends and of religious values. [The Pope Speaks, vol. 2 (1955) p. 367.]

Chapter 12

steps in selecting audio-visual equipment

PIERRE BABIN

What materials should be bought first? This question is often asked and is difficult to answer. In this age of extremely rapid technical mutation, we must always reckon with the sudden appearance of new products which will quickly alter the Audio-visual market.

Options dependent upon unforseeable developments

As we put the finishing touches to this book, two very important questions concerning the selection of equipment remain undecided for us:

1) Should we favor the cassette recorder or stay with the earlier reel-type recorder? While we prefer the latter for its seemingly broader range of effective uses, nevertheless the convenience of the cassette is undeniable. An indication of the popularity is the fact that the commercial market, particularly in the U.S.A. is flooded with inexpensive and excellent cassette recordings.

2) Should we invest heavily in filmstrips and slide-projection equipment, or wait for the commercialization of recent advances in video tape and other EVR equipment? At the present time, slide-projection equipment seems preferable, since it appears to have more appeal for adolescents. Slides speak to them in a more original way, and the pictures they will later recall are not ordinarily the "moving" ones. Besides, the quality of slide projections can hardly be matched by today's EVR equipment. Here again, a definitive choice is impossible; who knows what will be available on the market within the next few years.

Basic options

Another problem to be considered is the cost of the equipment. Is it right to invest so much money in audio-visuals? Is such equipment really necessary for effective catechesis, or are we just catering to a whim, giving in to a fad requiring a new style of expression? The answer to that question depends to a great extent on each individual's practical approach to education. However, it may be important to recall the following points:

The catechetical option to buy audio-visual equipment must be based more upon its effectiveness as a liberating force than upon mere personal taste. If I cannot justify my expenses by showing that I am educating young people or other educators to be more effective in the salvation of mankind, then perhaps I should not even entertain the thought of purchasing an expensive camera or projection equipment. What I buy must truly have an educational purpose. And this includes a genuine concern for the ignorant and voiceless masses, and for the Third World; indeed, to express and amplify what these people are living is part of any education.

In catechetics, many language-styles are possible: these include the traditional lecture form, student-teacher dialogue, books, films, and many more. Not all catechists can use these various styles with equal success. Each must therefore equip himself according to his personal talents and abilities. The teaching aids chosen should not exceed any individual's particular catechetical potential.

Moreover, a distinction should be made between the basic equipment that could be used by a school or parish, and the materials that would belong to a regional or diocesan center. It is important that these larger centers be appropriately equipped. They should be able to loan out materials and organize workshops for the formation of educators. Good equipment seems essential if the basic level of audio-visual education is to improve. It is not with cheap gimmickery that we can hope to educate; a minimum of quality is absolutely required.

Selection of equipment

Having made the above distinctions and reflections, the following suggestions concerning the choice of equipment are offered. The selection here, of course, is not concerned with specific makes of equipment, but with the steps in acquiring suitable instruments and materials.

First step: photos and pictures

The first step is to gather photos and pictures, classifying them according to themes.[1] These materials can be taken from many sources, such as magazines (e.g., *Life, Popular Photography*), photo collections (e.g. *Photolanguage, Symbolical Photos*), and albums (e.g. *Photography Annual*). Pictures chosen should not only be illustrative or descriptive, but also suggestive and symbolical.[2]

The educator himself should have a good camera, that is, one meeting these minimum requirements: variable lens (f-2.8 to f-16), changeable exposure (from 1/500 to 1 second, plus B), and focusing that can vary from 1 foot to infinity. The camera should be such that close-up attachments can be added to it to

[1] Suggested outlines for the classification of such material may be found at the end of this chapter.

[2] Picture selection techniques can, of course, vary. We suggest those found in P. Babin, et al., *Photolanguage* (Ottawa: The Catholic Centre of Saint Paul University, 1969 and Dayton, Ohio: Pflaum).

photograph periodicals, T.V. pictures, books, etc.

Second step: audio-visual montage

The basic equipment for any production of audio-visual montage consists of: a tape recorder (in some cases a record player will suffice) and a projector for slides or movie film. This basic equipment can be constantly improved. A record player with a good turntable and changer, a professional-type tape recorder, and a slide projector with remote control and automatic loading and focusing will prove invaluable in the production of a montage.[3] The ordinary white screen, while adequate, does not have the sharpness of a beaded one. The beaded screen, however, usually reflects the picture in a narrow angle, thus limiting audience size. A telescreen is what seems most appropriate: it allows for projection from behind the screen and gives a bright image even in a lights-on situation.

If slides are being collected, the regular 35mm type should be used, and this for uniformity and ease of classification, as well as for availability of projection equipment.

Catechetical AV centers should have all the above-mentioned equipment, and more. In fact, their recording equipment should have dubbing facilities, that is, the capacity to record sound on sound (synchro-play) or sound with sound (multiplay), and an adequate sound mixer. Besides this, the center should have a lending library containing some quality montages that could encourage others to produce their own; a collection of slides, photos, and films, and source material (books, pamphlets, periodicals) giving technical and artistic information.

Third step: television production[4]

Videotape or other E.V.R. equipment will be needed here, as well as a closed-circuit television hookup.

Fourth step: production of feature films

---

[3]Equipment even more sophisticated than this exists. For example, some projectors leave no dark or flashing gap between individual slides; others change slides automatically at a signal given from the soundtrack.

[4]Steps three and four are simply mentioned here, since they are really beyond the scope of this book. But the progression is important: step two, when well done, is a necessary apprenticeship for steps three and four, especially since it requires the preparation of a script and the fusing of the various audio-visual elements. Steps three and four require the use of much more elaborate equipment.

Classification of photos and slides

Efficient classification of visual materials allows for rapid filing and locating when they are needed. Headings should be relatively few in number, but precise and accurate as well as functional, that is, adapted to the goal at hand—in this case, religious education. Such a filing system will probably include at least three major divisions: themes, multivalent documents, and collections.

1. Thematic classification

Materials collected here will be related to a theme relevant for the religious education of youth. They either express a situation or suggest a possible answer or avenue of inquiry. Subheadings and cross-indexing can be added where desirable or necessary. The following is a suggestion for the development of such a classification:

a) Man and society

—the ages of man

—the key gestures and attitudes of man

—the inner conflicts of man

—human relations: man and woman, friendship, love, sex, the group, the gang, the crowd

—leisure: sports, recreation, music, food, T.V., books

—violence and suffering: hunger, conflict, tragedy, underdevelopment, war, racism, social struggle, injustice, death, strikes, riots

b) Man at work

—man and woman at work

—conquests of man: in the fields of science and technology, space travel, medicine

—education: illiteracy, adult education, job retraining

—communications: mass media

—transportation

—technology: computers, electronics

c) Man: culture and environment

—art, music, folklore
—geography, natural environment

—animal life

—biblical culture: historical, geographical, and other materials related to the Bible, the Gospel, Salvation History

—personalities: people who have shaped human thought or history, universal or local

—religion: attitudes, cults, beliefs, practices

d) Basic human situations

This heading is really beyond the scope of a thematic classification: it is in fact a cross-reference file enabling the user to rapidly find a series of symbolic or suggestive documents expressing the various problems or situations of today's man. This area of the classification should contain only the essential documents; only those photos or pictures which have a decided impact on young people should be filed here. Too much overlapping of materials can be easily avoided by adequate cross-indexing.

The photos filed here will evoke the great moments, the typical gestures, the significant actions and situations, the deep emotions, and so forth, which express most strikingly the life of modern man. Headings such as **anxiety, birth, compassion, death,** and **love, money, nature, pain, pleasure,** might be suitable here. If the photos chosen for this section are good, they will truly symbolize modern man's life and the meaning he gives to it, his basic aspirations and orientations, his need for identity and participation. For example, the picture of a man drinking at a bar could be filed under "leisure"; but it can also find its place here under "anxiety" because of his expression. Or the photo of an abandoned car my be classified under "death" or "solitude" because of what it symbolizes and expresses.

2. Polyvalent or multiuse materials

Here should be classified those photos and pictures which, while maybe lacking form and meaning in themselves, are however evocative and symbolic: photos of collages (e.g. children of many lands), natural symbols (e.g. the skeleton of a tree), symbolic expressions (e.g. haggard eyes), modern art (e.g. splashes of color, geometric designs, modern stained-glass, serigraphs).

For example, in creating an audio-visual montage on death, a fire or a barren tree could be used as symbols of what lies beyond, even though they are not directly linked with the death theme. In a similar way, a picture of broken and tangled lines could create a transition in a montage, giving the spectator an impression of confusion or even crisis.

Classification of this material will normally come under the following headings: graphics (collages, geometric designs, serigraphs, titles), nongraphic art (color here is the most important element), natural symbols (classified according to object pictured, e.g., tree, water, fire, etc.), symbolic expressions (e.g., eyes, hands, etc.).

3. Collections

Practically speaking, it is easier to recall pictures or slides when they are part of a series or collection. Thus, if a montage is worth keeping for a period of time, its pictures and slides should be kept together as a unit. The same must be said of series or collections that are precise and already well indexed, e.g., some UNESCO albums containing slides and explanatory booklet. It will be by far preferable to file these as units rather than to break them up in order to classify them according to themes or symbols.

bibliography

A. General Introduction to the Mass Media Culture

COLEMAN, Francis J. (editor), **Contemporary Studies in Aesthetics.** New York, McGraw-Hill, 1968.

DWORKIN, Martin S., "Aesthetics in Education" in **Journal of Aesthetic Education.** January 1968, pp. 21-29.

HURLEY, N. P., "The First Decade of the Noosphere," in **AMERICA,** vol. 117 (1967), pp. 171-173.

KEPES, Gyorgy (editor), **Education of Vision.** New York, George Braziller, 1965.

KUHNS, W., **The Electronic Gospel: Religion and Media.** New York, Herder & Herder, 1969.

LANGER, Susanne, "The Cultural Importance of the Arts." **Journal of Aesthetic Education I,** Spring 1966, pp. 5-12.

McLUHAN, H. M., **The Gutenberg Galaxy: the Making of Typographic Man.** Toronto, University of Toronto Press, 1962.

McLUHAN, H. M., **Understanding Media, the Extensions of Man.** New York, McGraw-Hill, 1964.

McLUHAN, H. M., **Verbi-voco-visual Explorations.** New York, Something Else Press, 1967.

McLUHAN, H. M. & FIORE, Q., **The Medium is the Massage.** New York, Random House, 1967 (also in paperback: New York, Bantam Books).

ONG, W., ed., **Knowledge and the Future of Man.** New York, Holt, Rinehart & Winston, 1968.

SONTAG, Susan, **Against Interpretation and Other Essays.** New York, Dale Publishing Co., 1966.

WHITE, D. M. & AVERSON, R., **Sight, Sound and Society.** Boston, Beacon Press, 1968.

Proceedings of First National Conference on Visual Literacy. Clarence M. Williams & John L. Debes (editors), New York, Pitman Corp., 1970.

Useful and stimulating articles on the communications media will be found in **AMERICA,** especially from such contributors as N. P. HURLEY (see above) and J. McLAUGHLIN.

B. Initiation into Audio-Visual Language

Sociological and Pedagogical Literature

BRADLEY, W. L., **The Meaning of Christian Values Today.** Philadelphia, Westminster Press, 1964.

CASSIRER, H. R., **Television Teaching Today.** New York, UNESCO, 1962.

GESSNER, R., **The Moving Image: a Guide to Cinematic Literacy.** New York, E. P. Dutton, 1968.

LINDGRENN, E., **The Art of the Film.** New York, Macmillan, 1963.

SCHILLACI, A., **Movies and Morals.** Notre Dame, Ind., Fides, 1968.

SKORNIA, H. J., **Television and Society: an Inquest and Agenda for Improvement.** New York, McGraw-Hill, 1965.

SOHN, D. A., **Film, The Creative Eye.** Dayton, Ohio, Pflaum, 1970.

MORRIS, M. & SAUERS, D., **And-Or.** New York, Harper & Row, 1968.

SPAAK, P. A. et al., **Man and His World: Terre des Hommes.** Toronto, University of Toronto Press, 1967.

STEICHEN, E., ed., **The Family of Man.** New York, Simon & Schuster, 1955.

SZARKOWSKI, J., **The Photographer's Eye.** New York, New York Graphic Society, 1966.

Periodicals will be particularly good sources of information and documentary materials. Among them:

CAMERA. Official organ of FIAP (International Federation of Photographic Art). A monthly publication originating in Switzerland.

THE CANADIAN AUDIO-VISUAL REVIEW. Published under the auspices of The Educational Media Association of Canada.

THE CANADIAN COMPOSER. Published by Creative Arts Co.

CANADIAN PROFESSIONAL PHOTOGRAPHY.

GRAPHIS. International journal of graphic and applied art published every two months by Editions Paralleles, 172 rue Pelleport, 75 - Paris 20, France.

MODERN PHOTOGRAPHY. A monthly review published by Billboard Publications.

POPULAR PHOTOGRAPHY. A monthly review published by Ziff-Davis Publishing Co., One Park Avenue, New York, New York 10016, U.S.A.

STEPHENSON, R., & DEBRIX, J. R., **The Cinema as Art.** Baltimore, Penguin Books, 1965.

VAIZEY, J., **Education for Tomorrow.** Baltimore, Penguin Books, 1966.

Some periodicals offer regular articles on audio-visuals; among these are the following:

THE LIVING LIGHT, 1312 Massachussetts Avenue, N.W., Washington, D.C. 20005, U.S.A.

THE RELIGION TEACHER'S JOURNAL, 904 Anthony Wayne Bank Building, Fort Wayne, Indiana 46802, U.S.A.

Contemporary Photography

BONI, A., ed., **Photographic Literature.** Hastings-on-Hudson, N. Y., Morgan & Morgan, 1962 (also: New York, R. R. Bowker).

LYONS, N., ed., **Contemporary Photographers Three: Vision and Expression, A Survey of International Photography.** New York, Horizon Press, 1969.

LYONS, N., ed., **Photography in the Twentieth Century.** New York, Horizon Press, 1967.

McMAHON, E. M. & CAMPBELL, P. A., **Please Touch.** New York, Sheed & Ward, 1969.

Two other publications by the editors of **Popular Photography** will also be of considerable interest:

PHOTOGRAPHY ANNUAL. Yearly. Ziff-Davis Publishing Co.

PHOTOGRAPHY DIRECTORY AND BUYING GUIDE. Yearly. Ziff-Davis Pub.

Popular magazines such as **ESQUIRE, LIFE, LOOK, PACE, THE UNESCO COURIER** will furnish the educator with wide-ranging examples of photographic art and will also supply him with many pictures that can be used in religious education.

Film Study

BERGMAN, I., **A Film Trilogy.** New York, Orion Press, 1967.

BOBKER, Lee R., **Elements of Film.** New York, Harcourt, Brace & World, Inc., 1969.

FEYEN, Sharon (editor), **Screen Experience: An Approach to Film.** Dayton, Ohio, Geo. A. Pflaum Publisher, 1969.

FISCHER, E., **The Screen Arts: a Guide to Film and Television Appreciation.** New York, Sheed & Ward, 1960.

HALLIWELL, L., The **Filmgoer's Companion.** London, McGibbon & Kee, 1967.

HODGKINSON, Anthony W., **Screen Education.** New York, Unesco Publications, 1964.

JACOBS, Louis, **The Emergence of Film Art.** New York, Hopkinson & Blake, 1969.

KUHNS, W. & STANLEY, R., **Exploring the Film.** Dayton, Ohio, Pflaum, 1969.

LYNCH, W. F., **The Image Industries: a Constructive Analysis of Films and Television.** New York, Sheed & Ward, 1959.

McANANY, E. G. & WILLIAMS, R., **The Filmviewer's Handbook.** Paramus, N.J., Paulist-Newman, 1965.

SAMUELS, Charles Thomas (editor), **A Casebook on Film.** New York, Van Nostrand, Reinhold, 1970.

SCHILLACI, Anthony, and CULKIN, John (editors), **Films Deliver.** New York, Citation Press, 1970.

The following publications will also be most useful in film study:

FILM CANADIANA (Canadian Film Institute, 1762 Carling Avenue, Ottawa 13, Ontario, Canada). A national, bilingual filmography, documenting all Canadian-produced films and T.V. programs and all films released in Canada for theatrical, non-commercial or television use.

FILMFACTS (1815 H Street N.W., Washington, D.C. 20006, U.S.A.). Published every two weeks with the collaboration of the American Film Institute. **Filmfacts** lists credits, synopses and critical reviews of all films released in the U.S.A., and publishes a yearly list of all awards given.

MEDIA MIX Newsletter, SCHRANK, Jeff (editor). Eight times a year, $6.00, Geo. A. Pflaum Publisher, Dayton, Ohio.

SEE Magazine, GIARRIZZO, Sal (editor). Six issues per year, $5, Geo. A. Pflaum Publisher, Dayton, Ohio.

SIGHT AND SOUND. International quarterly of the British Film Institute. Describes films produced or released in Great Britain.

C. Initiation into Audio-Visual Techniques

BABIN, P., et al., **Photolanguage.** Ottawa, Novalis, 1969, and Dayton, Ohio, Pflaum.

DALGLISH, W. A., **Media for Christian Formation.** 2 vols. Dayton, Ohio, Pflaum, 1969.

KUHNS, W., **Short Films for Religious Education.** Dayton, Ohio, Pflaum, 1967.

KUHNS, W., **Themes: Short Films for Discussion.** Dayton, Ohio, Pflaum, 1970.

McCAFFREY, P. J., **A Guide to Short Films for Religious Education Programs.** Notre Dame, Ind., Fides, 1967.

McCAFFREY, P. J., **A Guide to Short Films for Religious Education II, Including Some Experiences with Use of Film.** Notre Dame, Ind., Fides, 1968.

Audio-Visual Aids for High School Religion Classes. Winona, Minn., St. Mary's College Press, 1967.

CAVE NEWSLETTER (53 Park Place, New York, N.Y. 10008): a helpful monthly published by the Catholic Audio-Visual Educators Association.

Both the **National Education Association** (Audio-Visual Instruction Department) and UNESCO publish a number of works on the production and use of audio-visuals, especially in the field of education.

D. Resources for Audio-Visual Education

Bibliographical material

DILLON, J. T., ed., **Catechetics Reconsidered: Readings in Catechetics for High School Teachers.** Winona, Minn., St. Mary's College Press, 1968 (Part 5: Materials and Methods, pp. 161-189).

GRABOWSKI, S. M., "Using films in teaching religion," in **THE LIVING LIGHT** (Winter 1965-66), pp. 48-57.

HEYER, R., et al., **Discovery in . . .** New York, Association Press, and Paramus, N.J., Paulist-Newman. An interesting series, focusing on such areas as advertising, art, drama, film, literature, press, song, word.

Audio-Visual Resource Guide. New York, National Council of Churches of Christ in the U.S.A.

FILMS (The National Catholic Office for Motion Pictures, 405 Lexington, Avenue, New York, N.Y. 10017): a comprehensive review of the year in motion pictures.

Several centers provide booklets, critical notes and newsletters; among these:

The Catholic Adult Education Center (1307 South Wabash Avenue, Chicago, Illinois 60605).

Mass Media Ministries (2116 N. Charles Street, Baltimore, Maryland 21218).

National Center for Film Study (1307 South Wabash Avenue, Chicago, Illinois 60605).

Religion Teachers Association (3441 North Ashland Avenue, Chicago, Illinois 60657).

Saint Clement's Film Association (423 West 46th Street, New York, N.Y., 10036).

General Resource Centers

To the resource centers already mentioned in the above bibliographical guides, the following could be added:

American Bible Society (1365 Broadway, New York, N.Y., 10023).

Anglican Book Centre (600 Jarvis Street, Toronto 5, Ontario, Canada).

Argus Communications (3505 North Ashland Avenue, Chicago, Illinois, 60657).

Associated Visual Service Ltd. (1590 West 4th Avenue, Vancouver, B.C., Canada).

Association Films (135 Peter Street, Toronto 2B, Ontario, Canada).

Audio-Visual Education Library (10041 - 101 Street, Edmonton, Alberta, Canada).

Canadian Film-Maker's Distribution Centre (Room 312, Rochdale College, 341 Bloor Street West, Toronto 181, Ontario, Canada).

Cathedral Films (2921 West Alameda Avenue, Burbank, Calif., 91505).

Diadem Film & Supply Co. Ltd. (76 Sheppard Avenue West, Willowdale, Ontario, Canada).

Evangelical Publishers (4 Alberta Street, Toronto 1, Ontario, Canada).

Faith and Life Film Library (Box 430, Rosthern, Saskatchewan, Canada).

Gospel Supplies Ltd. (10016 - 101A Avenue, Edmonton, Alberta, Canada).

Missionary Audio-Visual Center (373 East Broadway, Vancouver 10, B.C., Canada).

National Council of Catholic Men (Communciation Dept., 405 Lexington Avenue, New York, N.Y., 10017).

National Film Board (P.O. Box 6100, Montreal 101, Quebec, Canada): the catalogue lists all of NFB's Canadian distribution centers.

Paulist Productions (17575 Pacific Coast Highway, Pacific Palisades, Calif., 90272).

Roa's Films (1696 North Astor Street, Milwaukee, Wisconsin, 53202).

Saint Francis Productions (1229 South Santee Street, Los Angeles, Calif., 90015).

Sovereign Film Distributors Ltd. (277 Victoria Street, Toronto, Ontario, Canada).

Sterling Movies Inc. (4980 Buchan Street, Montreal, Quebec, Canada).

United Church of Canada (Distribution Services, 85 St. Clair Avenue East, Toronto 7, Ontario, Canada).

Valley Audio-Visual Ltd. (1280 Wellington, Ottawa, Ontario, Canada).

Allen B. Wilson Guidance Associates. (Pleasantville, N.Y., 10570).

Feature Film Centers

A fairly complete list can be found in **Movies and Morals**; the following should be added:

Astral Films Ltd. (3811 Edmonton Trail, Calgary, Alberta; 5800 Monkland Avenue, Montreal, Quebec; 224 Davenport Road, Toronto, Ontario; 162 Union Street, Saint John, New Brunswick; 2182 West 12th Avenue, Vancouver, B.C.; 435 Berry Street, Winnipeg, Manitoba).

Canfilm Screen Service Ltd. (#201, 2312 - 4th Street S.W., Calgary, Alberta; 956 Richards Street, Vancouver 9, B.C.; 1790 St. Matthews Avenue, Winnipeg, Manitoba).

Cinemacraft (12456 De-Serres, Montreal 9, Quebec, Canada).

Columbia Pictures (72 Carlton Street, Toronto, Ontario; also in Calgary, Montreal, St. John, Vancouver, and Winnipeg).

Family Theatre Productions (7201 Sunset Boulevard, Hollywood, Calif., 90046).

International Film Distributors Ltd. (20 Bloor Street West, Toronto 5, Ontario, Canada).

Janus Film Library Ltd. (224 Davenport Road, Toronto 5, Ontario).

Paramount Film Service Ltd. (230 - 8th Avenue S.W., Calgary, Alberta; 5887 Monkland Avenue, Montreal, Quebec; 111 Bond Street, Toronto 2, Ontario; 45 King Street, Saint John, New Brunswick).

Sound, Recordings

See **Media for Christian Formation** for a list of records useful for educational purposes; similar information can be obtained from:

Youth Corps Program (Bond Street, Toronto, Ontario, Canada).

10071/7.5MV1170